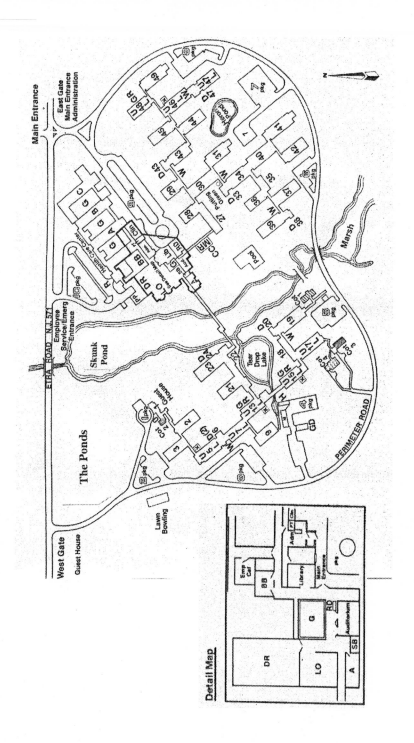

Second Chance

Life Inside
a Continuing Care
Retirement Community

Robert K. Scripps, Ph.D.

Copyright © 2004 by Robert K. Scripps

ISBN 0-7414-2145-3

Published by:

PUBLISHING.COM

1094 New DeHaven Street, Suite 100
West Conshohocken, PA 19428-2713
Info@buybooksontheweb.com
www.buybooksontheweb.com
Toll-free (877) BUY BOOK
Local Phone (610) 941-9999
Fax (610) 941-9959

Printed in the United States of America

Printed on Recycled Paper

Published February 2005

Table of Contents

Introduction

The Ponds is not an ordinary retirement community, it is a unique collective of highly accomplished individuals who have chosen to live their final years in a peaceful and comfortable setting in the company of others like themselves. This book offers an intimate portrait of that community and its residents, and it addresses the manner in which these residents, as Clifford Geertz puts it, "...[have] actually represented themselves to themselves and to one another." The large majority of those living at the Ponds at the time of this study were well over 80 years old and, as is typical of their cohort group generally, most had been outside of the "mainstream," socially and professionally, for some time.

One of several reasons for my interest in this particular population was my belief that its members might – because of their former pre-eminent social and professional statuses – have developed unique ways of adjusting to their presumed loss of defined roles in mainstream society. The research was conducted over a period of twelve weeks, during which I lived at the Ponds as a resident and, simultaneously, as a "participant observer".

In the spring of 1991, as a 50-year-old, almost retired broadcasting executive and a Ph.D. student in a cultural anthropology program, I was preparing for the required in-residence summer fieldwork. I was at about the two year mark at that point; the course work was drawing to a close, and it was necessary for me to figure out exactly what "culture" I wanted to study and where I wanted to study it. What I came up with was "elderly", and "nearby".

The "where" part was fairly easy given my age, my circum-stances as a family man, my business, and my wife's resistance to relocation. With those parameters, the research locale had to be here in the Northeast where I live, or at least near here, not, for example, in the Trobriand Islands or (more to my personal taste) in Boracay, Philippines. New Jersey was good...

Then there was the question of "whom" to study. How does one come to want to know more about how "the elderly" think about actually being "elderly", or about how they might describe themselves and their circumstance in a society such as ours? What, as we anthropologists say, are their systems of meaning? What are their ways of knowing?

My interest in the elderly, and particularly the "very old", is reasonably straightforward. I have always been intrigued by the aging process in terms of how one adjusts to one's changing "fit" (so to speak) with society and all that that must entail. What better way to find this out than by actually living with a "bunch" of "quite" (neither term academically defined) elderly individuals?

After numerous sessions with my academic advisor and a presentation of my proposed summer fieldwork to my second year colloquium group, I managed to get my field site approved by my department. I had decided on a Continuing Care Retirement Community (CCRC), because its population includes individuals in all of the developmental stages of very late life.

The average population of most CCRC's is around 85. A CCRC provides assisted living plus a complete in-house medical unit, including total care nursing. The idea is that one can "phase in" medical and other assistance as required. The assisted care is provided "cafeteria style", meaning that residents buy increments of time at an agreed upon rate, and utilize the time (i.e. the providers of the services) in the manner – such as assistance with bathing or dressing – which is most useful to them. The on-premises medical care and the assurance of a nursing bed (each resident is contractually

ii

guaranteed space in the nursing unit as needed) differentiates the CCRC from other types of assisted care living facilities.

During my course work I had also become interested in the notion of "disengagement". In 1961, two social scientists (Dr. Elaine Cumming and Dr. William E. Henry) published the results of a, "...detailed empirical study of a sample of older people and made what is probably the most serious attempt so far to put forward a general theoretical interpretation of the social and psychological nature of the aging process in America."

That study contains what has proved to be one of the most widely quoted and most heavily debated pieces of gerontological theory then or since; the notion of *disengagement*. In simple terms, when an elderly person "disengages" from society, she moves herself from its mainstream, creates new parameters and meanings for another lifestyle, and modifies the manner in which she interacts (or doesn't) with the society she has left behind.

Well, the academics, true to form, have jumped all over this. Some have chosen to study the "reasons" behind the alleged disengagement (loss of role in society, desire for freedom from role or gender constraints, making room for the next generation to take the helm, etc.). Some have chosen to attack the validity of the whole notion of disengagement.

Those taking this position propose instead that new, but equally vital roles (rather than the absence of roles) are culturally created for the elderly (e.g. keepers of the collective wisdom) resulting in a *de facto* "re-engagement" of mainstream society. Some have chosen to do cross-cultural comparisons of the roles and statuses of the elderly. Still others have chosen to address behavioral modifications resulting from such things as a more liberal interpretation of what is or isn't role appropriate. The literature is extensive.

In the case of the particular CCRC I had chosen for my research, the residents were quite interesting in that they were, for the most part, both highly accomplished professionally and at the upper end of the socio-economic scale. This, I felt, created the potential for unique variations from the "usual" processes of disengagement (or re-engagement or whatever variations surfaced) observed – or speculated about – by other researchers in other populations of the elderly.

Other things which interested me included a. the impact of the homogenous cohort group on the adjustment to very old age, and b. the role of reminiscence.

In the end, my primary research "problem" was to be, "…an attempt to identify and analyze the underlying social processes which act to maintain the equilibrium and sense of identity of a Continuing Care Retirement Community" [this quote taken from my post-study write- up]. In other words, I had positioned myself as trying to determine how (or even if) the elected CCRC, as a unique "community" of elderly individuals, goes about socializing its entering residents to a point where their membership in that community is one of the ways in which they begin to define themselves.

During the course of my stay at the Ponds I learned that I was not the only academic researcher to have done fieldwork there. A published Canadian sociologist specializing in gerontology had worked there in the 1980's with a focus on the process of death and what he refers to as the quest for a "successful life story" by those in their final years. Several residents still remembered him well, and I was offered the loan of the administration's copy of his research there.

This research was of great help to me in understanding some of the "rituals" of the place. I later found out that a number of the Ponds residents who had been there during that study were upset that the results were never released to the actual informants.

Additionally, a group of high school students working on a state grant, had done physical proficiency measurements and mobility studies on volunteers to determine such things as how long it takes an 80 something year old to cross a street. Residents still joked, at their own expense, about participating in experiments which they felt must have made them look ridiculous to this group of "youngsters".

I learned later from the head of the Resident Forum Committee that my research proposal had been accepted over one other – the contents of which I don't know – submitted by a psychiatrist.

What follows is an account of what I learned about this unique CCRC; how it was structured, how it was staffed, what people did there and what they had to say about it. It is hoped that the reader will come away with a sense of what it is like to live in this kind of place as a resident, and whether it is worth exploring as a retirement alternative.

Although this monograph is based upon research which was conducted according to the protocols of the academy and was originally produced to meet a particular academic objective, I feel that its contents have appeal – beyond the structural constraints and limited readership of the professional journal – for a larger audience. It should be of some interest to those who are looking at senior living alternatives for themselves or for other members of their families as well as those who are just plain curious about this unique style of living.

I have chosen to de-formalize the reporting of my experiences in this CCRC by replacing much of the arcane scholastic vernacular used in my original thesis with everyday language. My goal is to convey to the reader – in addition to an analysis of the objective experience – my personal feelings about and my reactions to the (often humorous) events and individuals I encountered there.

I have left in certain terms specific to the discipline, not to obfuscate, but to add a little academic "flavor" to the mix through the use of the phrasing that I was expected to utilize when addressing my scholarly peers. Also, some of these terms don't have synonyms, of more common usage, which convey the same nuances of meaning.

This writing does not purport to be representative in any way of the "typical" CCRC. The research was conducted in a manner which I feel can be replicated in other similar settings for further testing of the validity of my conclusions. I make no pretense here as to its possible acceptance as "general theory" about either the elderly or the aging process. I do not believe that any single ethnographic study should aspire to that status, and that is not my intention here.

Because the study population was a small one (330 residents and approximately 105 staff) living within readily definable boundaries, the scope of the study was well within the means of the single researcher. I was able to meet about 200 of these 330 Ponds residents and the majority of the staff.

I came to know almost half of the residents well enough I think to be accepted by them as a short term fellow "resident" in addition to a professional observer. And I developed an even deeper acquaintance with some in this smaller group, through repeated interaction, often in the relaxed, impromptu "social" setting (as opposed to a pre-scheduled interview, for example).

Members of the latter group became my "local friends", and they were to provide for me the large bulk of the material through which I was able to understand some of the "meanings" residents attach to their choice of the CCRC as a lifestyle. Although the people and places referred to herein are real, the names have been changed. The book is arranged as follows:

Chapter One provides a description of the Ponds physical layout, its history, and how I came to choose it as a site for my research. This chapter also provides a series of short profiles of the Ponds staff.

Rather than merely addressing job descriptions or job expectations, the attempt here is to bring the job holders to life as unique individuals apart from their functional responsibilities. I aspire to offer some insight into how they feel about themselves and the roles they play in this setting. I am also trying to convey how I believe that they feel about the residents as their clients and as their fellow actors.

In Chapter Two I discuss my entrance into the field site and how I spent the first couple of weeks there trying to sort things out and develop a strategy for "participant observation." I then describe how a typical day goes for the Ponds resident in terms of activities, meals, social engagements etc. Resident committees, local politics, symbolism and rituals (particularly those associated with food) are addressed in Chapter Three.

Chapter Four attempts an understanding of the notion of the downsizing of physical and social space which is mandated by the CCRC lifestyle. The chapter also highlights residents' fascination with nature and with their de-ritualization of death, phenomena which I have observed with other populations of this age group.

Chapters Five through Nine profile a number of Ponds residents who became critical to my research. This is an effort to add a "human" dimension to the foregoing 'macro' view of the community. The focus is upon that particular group of extraordinary individuals – my primary informants

- with whom I built my closest acquaintance, and without whom this study would have amounted to nothing more than a mundane, quasi-statistical survey. For this purpose I have employed biographical and autobiographical materials as revealed in selected excerpts from my many hours of conversations with these individuals.

I have chosen to divide these individuals into five groupings based upon such factors as length of residency, involvement with and status in (or acceptance by) the community, and former social and professional associations. I have "assigned" each of the key informants to one of these five categories based upon my perception of their commonality with others within their assigned group (i.e. as to behavior, stated opinions, allegiances, influence, community participation and so on).

The groups are not mutually exclusive, and many of the individuals fit comfortably into more than one category. The titles I have chosen for these groups are: The Original Settlers (Chapter Five), The Village Elders (Chapter Six), The New Turks (Chapter Seven), The Real Guest (Chapter Eight) and the Outliers (Chapter Nine). These designations are not entirely whimsical in that they reflect, in varying degrees, the behaviors, attitudes and relative statuses (i.e. vis-à-vis the community) of those within each group.

Finally, In Chapter Ten I take a look at whether my field work has produced enough empirical evidence to support my original research problem: the manner in which the community "socializes" or fails to socialize its new members. The chapter also provides some advice as to locating the "right" CCRC and as to preparing one's self for the CCRC lifestyle.

Chapter One

The Facts About The Place
And The Administrators & The Caregivers

The History:

The Ponds is a Continuing Care Retirement Community located in a small town named Hightown, which is about half way between Philadelphia and New York City. According to 95 year old resident Nettie Schutz, who was also born and raised in Hightown, the area's only significant industry prior to the 1950's was farming, mainly grain farming. During the 1950's, after the construction of a rail link from Hightown to New York City, several Fortune 500 Corporations built plants and office complexes in the area, and the town began to evolve from a rural village to an upscale suburban bedroom community.

The Ponds began operation in 1965 as a non-profit corporation owned by The Christian Community at the Ponds (CCP) which is a subsidiary of Christian Communities of New Jersey (CCNJ). CCNJ owns and operates nine facilities for the elderly, including nursing homes, apartment buildings, and life care facilities of both the full and modified service types. The original Ponds mission was to provide retirement residences and nursing care for moderate income individuals, mainly retired educators and other social servants.

A charter Ponds resident told me, however, that even in its early days, there was a contingency of affluent residents from Westchester County, New York living here. It is the oldest full service life care facility on the East Coast. As a full service facility, residents are, "...provided with and/or offered personally-selected living units, general medical and nursing care, meals, housekeeping, utilities, transportation and other services."

The Ponds has had its ups and downs since its inception. When I began my research, it had had seven directors over the course of its 24 years of existence, but only one, Jim Daniels, the current Director (a former banker), had had any real experience in management. Another Ponds resident, Mrs. Lovins told me that, with one exception, all of the Directors prior to Jim had been Protestant ministers with no experience outside of the church. The first Director of Grounds and Maintenance had been a retired high school football coach and the second was a former farmer whose staff consisted of 5 manual farm laborers.

Ponds operating costs grew rapidly, and the original projections of life expectancy - based upon actuarial tables available at the time - had been far too conservative. Dr. Yount, the Ponds medical director, told me that he felt that the stress-free, relatively luxurious lifestyle led by the residents here was a major contributing factor to their increased longevity. The upshot was that the income from residents had to be increased dramatically and the socio-economic demographics of the place began to change.

Fees were soon out of reach for all but the more affluent, and the age of the average resident had increased significantly. Due to this, quite a few of the original residents left the community. The older, more affluent residents became less involved in the day to day affairs of the facility. Many felt that they had already made their contributions to society, and they were now focused on relaxation and life simplification.

Costs and Admissions:

The required minimum age for admission to the Ponds is 65, but according to the facility's Director, the average age of admission is approximately 80, and the average age of the resident group living there during my research was 84. The facility is equipped with a 90 bed total care nursing facility (approximately 80-85 of which are being utilized at any given time) and two full-time resident physicians (with a third slated to be hired shortly).

Depending upon the type of residence desired (they range from small studios without cooking facilities to spacious two bedroom detached cottages with all the amenities of a small home), entrance fees were between $50 and $275 thousand, while monthly maintenance/service fees ranged from $1,370 to over $4,700. This sliding scale of monthly fees, Marcie Jeanne Franklin., Ponds' Director of Marketing told me, is due to the fact that there are three contract levels available to entering residents. "A" contracts include all of the facility's available services; "B" contracts include a "bank" of basic services with "as used" fees thereafter; and "C" contracts provide a straight fee for services arrangement.

For residents entering the nursing facility, the monthly fee was $2,000 minus a deduction of 3% of the balance of the portion of the entrance fee, if any, which is returnable at the time of admittance to the health care unit. In-residence personal care is charged at the rate of $7.50 per quarter hour increment (the most often requested in-residence services at the Ponds, I learned from one of the RN's I ate my meals with, are "straightening up", bathing and putting on "thrombo-stockings").

By New Jersey State law, all of an individual's money has to be refunded if that individual changes his or her mind about entering a CCRC within 30 days of acceptance.Up to 50% a new resident's deposit is refundable on a sliding scale within the first two years of residency. Residence contracts are very detailed and quite complex, however, and various people advised me that those considering living in this type of facility should have contracts reviewed by an attorney specializing in elder law, before committing. The substantial up front deposits and monthly charges are obviously a major factor in defining the general socioeconomic circumstances of the resident group entering this type of upscale CCRC.

The Population:

The resident population at the time of my study was 330, living in 300 residential apartments. The permanent staff at the Ponds was 105 (this was supplemented by a varying number of temporary kitchen helpers, privately-contracted resident companions etc.). With the exception of several Asians, all of the residents of the Ponds were white. Most had lived formerly in greater Philadelphia, greater New York and central New Jersey. A significant minority, however, came from a diversity of geographic locations including Tokyo, St. Croix and Bermuda. In all, 79 U.S. cities, 17 U.S. states and three foreign countries (a number too were first generation immigrants from countries in Eastern and Western Europe) were represented in the community.

Occupationally, about a quarter of the residents were former executives of private corporations, 16% were from academia, 15% were from professional/government backgrounds, the arts or publishing. The other 44% were what I term the "non-occupational" group because they are hard to place into standardized professional categories. This group was composed almost solely of what might be referred to colloquially as "society ladies" – i.e. women who were married or had been married to prominent professional men.

Many of these women had been extremely active in volunteer work (social work, charities etc.), clubs (garden clubs, alumnae clubs, social clubs etc.; about 38% of the women at the Ponds during my residence fell into this category) and other endeavors which are not monetarily compensated.

The large majority of residents possessed at least a college degree. But what was particularly interesting to me was the significant number of women who had earned Ph.D. degrees in the 1920's and 1930's when only a minority of Americans even went to college.

Reflective of the general "category" of resident sought by the facility, Marcie Jeanne Franklin told me that, although the Ponds advertises regularly in the alumnae magazines of the Ivy League colleges, 80% of reservations, 58% of sales and 47% of all basic inquiries are referrals from current residents. This fact more or less assures the continuance of the existing resident composition.

Additionally, the Ponds marketers were thinking of ways to go after what she calls the "influencers" (i.e. the trust officers, attorneys, financial advisors etc. of residents who have the potential for referring other clients of the "desired" type). And they were also seeking to reach affluent members of the so-called "sandwich" generation (i.e. those middle-age people who are involved with the welfare of both their children and their elderly parents).

Of over 700 CCRC's in existence at time I was there, the Ponds was one of only 107 accredited by the American Association of Homes for the Aging. When this list is circulated as a public service, the Ponds receives important free publicity. As mentioned above, the average age of admission to the Ponds was about 80, with average resident age 84 (down from 86.7 just a few years prior). In terms of gender, approximately 85% were women, 15% men; 23% of residents were married couples. This worked out to a female to male ratio of five and a half to one, which was more than twice the national average for the U.S. population of people over 85.

The original capitalization and resident financing of the facility was based on actuarial estimates of life span for the

U.S. population at large as of 1965. This fact has caused financial difficulties for the community over the years because well cared-for, unstressed Ponds residents have far exceeded the life span expectations of the general population (particularly those projections formulated 25 years previously). The Canadian sociologist who studied the Ponds in 1968, quotes one of the residents as saying, "I've heard you get such beautiful care here you haven't a chance of dying. Here's the administration wanting you to die because they want to sell apartments, and the medical staff wanting you to live."

At the time of this study, the average life span at birth for white males and white females was approximately 69 and 77, respectively. At the Ponds, the corresponding ages were about 89 and 90. It seems possible that the small difference in age at death between males and females in this sample might be attributable to the fact that there were far fewer men than women in the community (and in this sample) and to the fact that the males who make it to the Ponds are the ones with longevity on their side. The men at death ranged in age from 73 to 99, while the women at death ranged in age from 73 to 103. Only five of the women in this sample (2.4%) and none of the men were at or below the national average at time of death.

The Physical Layout:

The atmosphere of the Ponds is one of quiet elegance, with over 100 acres of well-manicured grounds and natural woodlands, three man-made lakes and a beautiful old mansion - restored to its original opulence - which now serves as a twelve room guest house. The more than fifty individual buildings comprising the facility are connected by literally hundreds of yards of covered, climate-controlled, glass-sided hallways. I determined, by actually pacing it off, that it is approximately one fifth of a mile between the two furthest residence units.

A number of the other physical measurements of Ponds space which I use in this study, however, were provided to me by Mrs. Learner, a permanent resident of the nursing facility, who had measured virtually everything in the place and recorded it for Ponds posterity (she was also the person who informed me that the mailbox complex behind the reception desk is - properly - referred to as the "whirly-gig").

There are eight large day rooms, one for each residence wing. These rooms are designed for community entertaining (which can be fully catered by the Ponds dining room staff) and are equipped with their own kitchens. Each is luxuriously appointed (well-stocked bookcases, card tables, writing desks, many genuine antiques) and each has a large working fireplace.

The center of community activity, however, is the area I refer to as the "quadrangle" (quad). All of the residence wings (and the nursing care wing) are connected to the quad, and through the quad, to each other. The quad itself is a small courtyard which articulates with a grouping of community facilities including the library, a telephone operator/mailbox complex (the aforementioned "whirly-gig"), a large auditorium, a snack bar, a crafts room, the main lounge, the central dining room and a beauty parlor.

The primary administration offices are located behind the library, behind the corridor (referred to as "sunshine alley" because the permanent nursing care residents and other convalescents sit there during the day to take in the sun through the corridor's glass walls and ceiling) leading to the nursing care complex and the clinic. The employee cafeteria, the accounting offices and the social worker/resident affairs offices are also connected to the quad through another series of corridors leading toward the northeast corner of the property.

The 6,000 volume library was assiduously maintained by Helene Koster and Dr. Effie Brontman, both "Village Elders" (in charge of the main stacks and the archives, respectively), and Jeanne Sandler, a "New Turk" (in charge of the day room book shelves).

I had anticipated a preponderance of biographies and autobiographies in the Ponds reading materials because my predecessor, the Canadian sociologist, had reported the residents, who were focused on bringing their own life stories to successful conclusions, would be interested in the lives of others. What I found, however, was a broad mix of subject matter including everything from modern pulp fiction (e.g. lots of Sidney Sheldon) to the classics; just what I probably should have expected from a group with this sort of professional and cultural diversity.

There are 49 groupings of residence units extending out from the quad through two main corridors. The southwest corridor crosses the main lake, which is called Skunk Pond, and ultimately leads also to the maintenance buildings, the resident's shop and the community's greenhouse (which is shared, with a certain amount of friction, by the Ponds grounds staff and the residents). The Ponds grows all of its indoor plants and flowers.

As already mentioned, about 75% of the residence units are built at ground level. There are five floor plans available ranging from the basic studio to the large, two bedroom, two bath units. These large units are called "cottages". They are quite luxurious, and give the feeling of the small, unattached ranch homes one might encounter in a suburban community. All of the residence units have their own cooking facilities, and all have their own private verandas. Residence "owners" were soon to be given the option of enclosing these patio areas, at their own expense, in order to provide more living space.

The Ponds has a total of ten uncovered parking lots, including separate areas for visitors and employees. There are also a number of indoor and outdoor recreational facilities, including a lawn bowling court, an olympic-size swimming pool, three croquet greens (one indoors) and two exercise rooms. The architecture of the buildings is reminiscent of Frank Lloyd Wright, which is due to the fact that the architect who designed them for the Ponds was a former student of Wright's at Princeton.

The design produces ambient lighting both through large skylights and through floor-to-ceiling glass along each corridor. This, along with paint and carpeting in light pastel colors, has the effect of opening up the indoor common space and giving it a natural ambience reflective of the outdoor surroundings with which it articulates.

According to one resident interested in the history of the place, the corridors, grounds and recreation areas of the Ponds were designed for walking, with the idea of maintaining health and longevity through regular exercise. Additionally, the corridors are over ten feet wide, thus allowing for the comfortable passage of wheel chairs, the three-wheel carts used by non- or partially ambulatory residents and service vehicles (namely the large electric vehicles operated by health center employees for residence-administered personal care and emergency medical attention).

The design of the Ponds includes a number of safety features for its residents. There are frequent rest areas along the corridors containing comfortable couches, and varying arrangements of easy chairs and reading lamps. During my stay at the Ponds, I very rarely experienced a period of more than a couple of minutes in any of the common areas during normal daytime hours (from about 6 am to 9 pm) without encountering another individual, be it an employee or a resident.

Additionally, every telephone in every residence unit is equipped with an emergency button which rings at the main telephone desk; this happens automatically if the hand set of the telephone is not in use but is off the hook for more than a minute or two.

Even though the exteriors of all of the residence units are identical, many residents had personalized their front doors and the hallways immediately in front of their apartments. Doorways and adjacent hallways had decorative nameplates, or welcome mats, or wreaths, or brass umbrella stands, or arrangements of seasonal flowers.

And, as I was to find out during my in-residence interviews, the interiors of these apartments were often wondrously unique little sanctuaries. They were miniature replicas of former homes, crammed full of antiques and heirlooms like great grandmothers' dining room tables and couches or (shortened) grandfather clocks or prized oriental rugs. There were pictures of family and friends everywhere and mementos of college days and great grandchildren's artwork.

It struck me that these individuals were, quite successfully it appeared, hanging on to small pieces of their former identities, while at the same time adding a sort of neighborhood feel to the sterile sameness of these entrances and a cozy familiarity to the individuals' living quarters, reminiscence of the ones they had left behind.

The Administrators & The Caregivers

While at the Ponds I ate my breakfasts and lunches in the staff dining area. I developed a good rapport with this lively and varied group. I got to know many of them quite well, and through them I was provided with a unique view of the residents and the workings of the community. The staff perspective sometimes supported the conclusions I had arrived at through observation and through my interactions,

10

but, just as often, it presented reasonable alternatives to them.

Those who ate their meals in the employee dining room included the administrative staff (accounting, marketing, resident services, etc.), the maintenance workers, the medical staff (staff doctors, resident nurses and nurses aids) and a few of the residents' private nurses aids and companions.

Ponds residents interacted with some staff members on an almost a day to day basis, but had very limited contacts with others.

Many dealt with Jim both formally, as Director, and socially. Jim had become quite close to some of the residents who, from time to time, invited him to join them for lunch or dinner in the Ponds dining room. He was even invited to a few of the small cocktail parties in residents' apartments. The usual interactions, however, took place in committee meetings, impromptu run-ins in the Ponds common areas or at Ponds-sponsored social events such as the annual staff picnic and the Christmas party.

Some of Jim's department heads (e.g. Maggi Lane, the Controller, the resident physicians, Drs. Yount and Coburn, and Katie Bee, the Marketing Director/Admissions Coordinator) confined most of their interactions with residents to a purely professional level; service provider-client.

Others, however, (like Beth Hamlin, Resident Services Manager, and Debbie Dempsy-O'brien, Head Activities Director) held positions requiring extensive social interaction with residents. And, of course, the floor staff (companions, nurses, nurse's aids) were continuously addressing residents' day to day, often very personal, needs.

On my first day at the Ponds, Jim's administrative assistant, a young woman named Ellie Barns, informed me that the residents were,

> "...tough cookies, used to asserting themselves, managing people and having their way."

I later found that this point of view was one held by a number of Ponds staff members, including those who had formed warm relationships with some of the residents. Even staff members with these feelings toward certain residents, however, didn't generalize the sentiment to include the entire resident body. The usual situation was one in which a given staff member perceived some residents to be generally nice, unassuming people, while perceiving others to be "effete snobs" who felt themselves above the Ponds "working class."

Dr. Yount, who was the head staff doctor was formally trained as an internist, had become, through his own inclinations and his practical experience at the Ponds, a *de facto* geriatrician. He seemed extremely interested in and very well informed about issues arising from what has become known as "the graying of America". He had a number of concerns related to this evolving phenomenon, and it proved an easy matter for me to draw him into extended conversations about them.

Dr. Yount also appeared to have a genuine affection for his Ponds patients and a real interest in their psychological as well as their medical needs. As an example of this, he seemed to genuinely empathize with the sort of "separation anxiety" evidenced by a number of his regular patients each Friday when they knew the staff doctors would be gone for the weekend.

Dr. Yount also informed me that he was worried about the critical shortage of physicians trained to treat the elderly, because, he said,

"... the U.S. population is aging rapidly, and the supply of trained geriatrricians does not meet even the current demand. And I believe, as is currently the case, it is very dangerous for physicians not trained specifically in geriatric medicine to be treating the aged in the same manner as they treat their other adult patients. The elderly have very different levels of metabolism, lower tolerances for medication."

Dr. Yount. admitted the desirability of an intermediate care facility at the Ponds, but he said,

"It is a major decision which requires careful analysis as to how it would be financed and utilized. There are also more mundane problems such as town sewerage permits, state certification etc. to be addressed."

In regard to adding a third staff physician, my next question, I think that he may have been hesitant to discuss the matter because there was a budget issue vis-à-vis the Christian Homes administration, and he didn't know which side of the issue he would be called on to defend. He did tell me though,

"The former third Ponds doctor who left to go to another CCRC in the group was extremely popular with the residents, and they seem to feel that the administration had somehow 'stolen' her from them against her true wishes."

The nurses and nurses aides with whom I ate most of my breakfasts and lunches were not generally as guarded about or as sensitive to Ponds politics as Drs. Yount. and Coburn.

Most had a sort of "tell it as it is" attitude toward both their wards and their employer.

Nina Boyer is an RN who was assigned alternately to the total care facility and to the intermediate care (IC) "team" which provided in-residence medical attention (i.e. dispensing prescription medications, treating minor ailments, bathing those with mobility problems etc.). She was the jokester of the group. The four person IC contingency (Cindy Rogers, Barbara, Betsy Kleine. and Caitlyn Craig were the other members) utilized a modified electric golf cart to cover the Ponds widely dispersed residence units.

Because the IC unit members always seemed to be in a hurry, they wheeled around the corridors at high rates of speed relative to the elderly residents, who were moving about mostly on foot. Nancy told me, almost proudly, of several "traffic" accidents, one of which apparently involved running over a resident's foot. Due to complaints by residents, she was thought to be on Jim's alleged "list" of staff to keep an eye on.

Shirley Penrose (the white haired, rather matronly head nurse who told me that she had "seen it all" over her long nursing career), on the other hand, had a disciplined, almost motherly demeanor, at least until you got to know her. She became very friendly and talkative with me, because I think that she was interested in what I was doing. But her parental attitude also derived from the fact that she was being relied upon to assure that her younger, more exuberant charges maintained the decorum that was expected of that coterie of caregivers. Mrs. Penrose, who had been at the Ponds longer than most of her peers, provided a wealth of "inside" information to me about both its staff and its residents.

As with Nancy, the majority of the nursing and nurse's aid staff at the Ponds spoke quite openly about the personal lives of the residents in their care. Some floor staff were candid

14

with me about their dislike of certain residents. A number of the socially prominent female residents (like Rosalie Gardiner and Flow Harrison), who had done *pro bono* social work in their former communities seemed to feel that the Ponds floor staff could learn a few things from them. Nancy told me,

> "These ladies who are used to managing people and being in charge, try to assert themselves in volunteer work in the Health Care Unit. For example, Mrs. Barns wanted a clown at every birthday party. And Sarah Langley, the RN in charge of health care activities, told her that they would quickly get 'clowned out'. There are too many chiefs for the amount of work that has to be done."

When I ran into Beth Hamlin, an RN and Ponds Resident Services Administrator, in the hallway one afternoon, she told me,

> "One morning I saw two quite elderly spinsters in the laundry room who seemed totally baffled by the use of the washing machine and the fold down ironing board. These people never had to do any ironing before or any other menial tasks, and they had to learn how."

But even though they joked about them and complained about them continuously, it was obvious to me that floor staff felt a lot of affection toward the residents too. This was displayed on more than one occasion during my stay through the manner in which these staff members openly grieved the passing of favorite residents. Apropos to this, Mrs. Penrose told me,

> "I feel that being a geriatric nurse in a facility like this is mainly a maintenance function because the

diseases [Alzheimers, senility, fractures, tumors etc.] are largely recurring.".

Beth Hamlin was a slim, attractive brunette in her 40's with two grown children (a daughter with a Masters Degree in Art and a 20 year old son who was a college dropout and still "finding his way"), and a deceased husband. She told me,

"I came in contact with the Ponds 17 years ago when I was working as the private duty nurse for the wife of an internationally prominent economist. In this position I traveled around Europe and Asia. I came back to work at the Ponds six years ago as a 'paper pusher' in the social services department. I later worked for the Marketing Department, and I was only recently given my current job, which is actually the consolidation of two jobs because of the budget cuts."

Beth was popular with the Ponds staff (she had worked both in "operations" as a practicing RN and in corporate administration) and with the Ponds residents (she is an ex-caregiver who had worked with clientele similar to those residing at the Ponds).

Beth feels that most people came to the Ponds at a point when they felt they had no other option. She told me,

"They gave up their homes only when they had absolutely no other choice. Some felt they were giving the ultimate gift to their children by not asking them to be their caregivers. In spite of this, though even those who anticipate just whiling away their time and awaiting death, find that a whole new world evolves for them and that they often become livelier, clearer of mind and more energetic in the CCRC type of environment."

When I mentioned the "golden days" of the Ponds, she admitted that,

> "When I was here 17 year ago, residents didn't even dress themselves, they had their clothes laid out for them. And that the lounge used to be like a men's grill with dark wood and heavy leather chairs. "

When I mentioned complaints by some as to a lack of intellectual stimulation, she said,

> "No place can be all things to all people, and the elderly have to accept the fact that there is a point in the aging process when they have to give up some of the elements of their previous life styles".

As a former caregiver to the elderly, Beth was empathetic as to their needs and their concerns. She was a realist too, however, and she felt that, "Ponds residents are receiving the absolute best that money can buy".

As the head of the Ponds grounds and maintenance staff, Jerry Bradford was frequently caught between the demands of his boss Jim and the persistent requests for attention by the residents. Jim had his own ideas about many of the "small", routine matters under Jerry's jurisdiction, such as the replacing of spent light bulbs (he felt they should be replaced as soon as they burned out, whereas Jerry proposed changing burned out light bulbs on only one day each month – there's a classic business school problem for you!).

And Jim was the final authority as to how the budget money got spent, meaning that new equipment purchases, additional maintenance staff etc. were sometimes put on hold, in lieu of matters of higher corporate priority; regardless of Jerry's recommendations.

For Jerry there was an inherent, friction producing conflict of interest involved with the servicing of individual resident's maintenance requests - often perceived by those residents as "emergencies" requiring immediate attention - because these interfered with his normal crew scheduling, his overtime budget and his ability to meet project deadlines. To illustrate his predicament, Jerry told me,

> "I had once had a resident call me at 5:00p.m., just as I was wrapping things up for the day, to complain of an air conditioner that smelled. When I inspected the unit I couldn't detect any smell at all, and I told the resident that I wasn't about to schedule somebody for two hours overtime to solve a 'problem' that didn't exist. The resident demanded that it be fixed or he would report the incident to Jim. I told her to go ahead, 'maybe Jim can come over and fix it himself with his own little tool kit' ."

Jerry was an amiable guy and a lot of fun as a breakfast or lunch companion, but he had a bit of a 'gruff' streak and was probably not always as diplomatic as he could have been with this group of residents, who he felt to be both unaware of and unsympathetic to the extent of his responsibilities as Director of Grounds and Maintenance for a community the size of a small village.

The residents, in turn, took the view that because they had no other source of help when it came to getting things repaired, and because they were paying substantial monthly maintenance fees for the privilege of not having to deal with these problems, they were entitled to "on demand" priority service. In the final analysis, however, grounds and maintenance staff were generally well liked by the residents, the large majority of whom had no complaints about the quality of service they received.

As the head chef at the Ponds, Sal Trematossi had his hands full living up to the expectations of the facility's 300 plus would be gourmands, the majority of whom were accustomed to dining at some of their regions' finest restaurants. And then there was Melanie Kirk - former socialite and author of several well received books on the art of gastronomy (more about her in Chapter Six) – who was the head of the resident food committee.

Mrs. Kirk, brought up as a southern lady of leisure, had divorced her husband and sole source of livelihood a decade or so before entering the Ponds, and had proceeded to establish herself as a leading authority on the art of gracious entertaining. And she was very, very serious about her role in maintaining the dining standards of the Ponds.

If the situation had been confined to a one on one between Mr. Trematossi and Mrs. Kirk, it might have settled down into some sort of uneasy peace between the competing egos. But, Mrs. Kirk had several resident peers (e.g. Amber Wentworth, Merin Coulter and Helene Koster) who felt themselves to be at least her equal in the science of fine dining, and who felt they should, food committee members or not, have a say in the kitchen output and general goings on.

What resulted was a matrix of opinions, instructions, interactions and reactions between Mr. Trematossi and the various other participants, and between and among the other participants themselves. In spite of this, however, Mr. Trematossi managed to regularly deliver above average cuisine to the resident body.

It somehow seemed that many of the Ponds corporate department heads fell into one of two general types: the bureaucrats (or "paper pushers") and the "people" persons. The Ponds' Admissions/Marketing Coordinator and the Ponds' Social Coordinator, respectively, are representative examples of these two categories.

Whereas in the early years, the Ponds administration had placed much of its emphasis on issues of life quality and staff-resident relations, an equal emphasis now was placed on marketing the facility to healthy, economically upscale resident candidates. In the process of this shift in focus, one of the staff most beloved by residents - because of her active advocacy of their causes - had been forced to resign; she had failed to "deliver" her quota of new resident prospects.

This individual had been replaced by two new staff, one of whom was a "preppy" young suburbanite with a Masters in Social Work, named Katie Bee. Katie's title was Marketing/Admissions coordinator. She did most of the pre-screening of new applicants, and she worked with members of the marketing staff to recruit new residents, largely from current resident referrals and through advertisements in Ivy League college alumni publications.

Katie was one of the first people I met at the Ponds. She was pretty, very businesslike, and, I was to learn, extremely opinionated. I found her to be more of a statistics person than a people person, and I think that is what made her somewhat (quite in some cases) unpopular with a number of the residents. Katie asked me on more than one occasion to give her my opinions of various residents, and she was quite forthcoming with her own opinions about them (e.g. she found Helene Koster, the Ponds resident librarian, to be an "insufferable snob").

I feel that Katie was hoping to gain knowledge from me which would provide leverage for her to use against those who she regarded as 'troublemakers" (i.e. those who didn't fit the "desired" resident profile in terms of background, behavior, politics etc.). I learned to be extremely careful of what I said to or in front of Katie.

Conversely, Marcie Jeanne Franklin, the Ponds Resident Social Coordinator, had a warm, open relationship with most of the residents. Ms. Franklin had somewhat of an edge over Katie Bee in that she was comfortably into middle age and very socially outgoing. Her mother had been a Ponds resident up until her death several years prior to my stay, and Marcie Jeanne herself (she was on a first name basis with everyone there as far as I could tell) was looked upon by many as a (virtual) fellow resident and as a friend rather than as a staff member. She had been associated in one way or another with the Ponds since its inception, and, because she was from a "good" family and because she was both well educated and well traveled, she was a natural to assume her role as Social Coordinator.

Marcie Jeanne provided entertainment for the residents in the form of movies, speakers, day trips, in-house music performances and so on. But her crowning achievement was the series of overseas trips she arranged and chaperoned each year for those residents who were physically and financially able. Her favorite destination was France, because she herself loved the French culture and because France is where she met her husband. When I asked her about the difficulty of traveling with the very old, she told me that,

> "Travel with a group of elderly in tow requires full time attention, but it certainly is doable. I do, however, take the precaution of requiring, from each member of each entourage, medical verification of the ability to tolerate the stress of overseas travel."

In the following chapter I am attempting to describe for the reader what it was like for me when I first arrived, and what goes on there day to day.

Chapter Two

Entering The Field
And How the Day Goes

I arrived at the Ponds in early June with a car full of clothes, books, office supplies and a laptop computer with a compact printer. I headed for Jim Daniels' office where I was introduced to most of the administration department heads. Jim had been the Ponds Director for about two years at this point. Afterwards I had a quiet one-on-one lunch with Jim in the main dining room where he informed me that while living at the Ponds I was to pay a very low monthly rent for the use of a small studio which had been converted from staff office space.

I would eat, at my own expense (at the low, subsidized employee rate) with Ponds staff in the employee dining areas unless invited by a resident for a meal in the resident dining hall. I later found out that there was no objection to my eating in the resident dining room on my own and signing my room number for later billing.

Although my presence and the purpose of my research was pre-approved by the Ponds resident committee as well as by Ponds management, I was asked to speak about my project to the total resident body during one of their regularly scheduled Forum Committee meetings.

From the beginning of my stay I was generally well received by the Ponds community. The residents were polite to a fault, and several – mainly those whose careers had been in fields such as education, social services or social sciences – seemed very interested in both the objectives and the methodology of my proposed study. A number of these same individuals approached me after my introduction at the

Forum Committee meeting and offered to help me with my study.

Even with this friendly welcome, however, I felt quite awkward at first. I believe that I was suspected by some of the residents of being a "spy" (a stigma anthropologists seem to have to deal with from time to time) for Ponds management.

Similarly, management, although openly receptive to my undertaking, seemed to be somewhat wary of me for what they may have perceived as my potential for providing "bad press" for the establishment. My task, as I saw it, was to "blend in" in order to ferret out the "natives" point of view concerning themselves (or, as Clifford Geertz would say, "...to figure out what the devil they think they are up to."). I immedfiately set about developing a strategy to accomplish this objective.

The implementation of my strategy was to be delayed by a couple of weeks, however. My first week was spent in the company of Jim and his staff. I attended meetings with the management of other CCRC's in the area as well as internal Ponds staff meetings. I learned how Jim's group perceived the resident population at large and how they felt about specific individuals within it.

Among other things, Jim was quite concerned with what he referred to as, "the callous disregard" of some individuals for their fellow residents. This was mainly evidenced, he told me, in quality of life issues such as noise, use of community facilities, and a general insensitivity to the feelings or circumstances of others.

Because of this perception, Jim was working on methods - such as regular phone calls to housing units, check-in procedures for meals and activities, etc. - for assuring that nobody was overlooked during times of need. He also informed me of how he felt that his "team" was perceived by the residents. Jim was aware, for example, that residents blamed him for their absence of representation on the Ponds board of directors and for allegedly allocating the fees received from Ponds residents to other CCRC's within this Protestant group.

During my second week at the Ponds, I was invited to attend a meeting of selected department heads from a consortium of CCRC's. The meeting was attended by General Directors, Medical Directors, Marketing Directors and Resident Services Directors (nursing and social services). As mentioned in the previous chapter, I learned from the Ponds marketing people that approximately three quarters of the residents had chosen this CCRC through word of mouth recommendations from friends, and that virtually the only medium used to advertise the facility is Ivy League alumni association publications.

In line with this, I also found that social "cliques" within the resident body contained many who had known each other throughout their working careers (some even since childhood), had attended the same colleges, lived in the same suburbs, belonged to the same clubs etc.

The rising costs of medical care is the single biggest financial problem for the Ponds (and CCRC's in general I would venture). On the one hand they want to maintain the main advantage they offer over other types of retirement facilities (i.e. their full service medical care), but on the other, they don't want to price themselves out of the market.

One of the marketing directors stated to the group that she considers the ideal resident to be one who, "enters residence, doesn't 'gobble up' a lot of services, lives three months and dies". Somewhat at odds with this sentiment it seemed to me, however, was the current Ponds marketing slogan, "come early", which was designed to attract a younger (and presumably healthier) resident body. I was soon to find out why these concerns prevailed within the group.

All of the CCRC's represented at this meeting maintained elaborate entrance selection procedures to narrow the odds of admitting residents who might become expensive to "maintain". In the case of the Ponds, entry involved five steps: 1. A preliminary screening by Katie Bee, head of social services, to determine potential compatibility with the Ponds lifestyle (a.k.a. the Ponds "image"), 2. A questionnaire filled out by the applicant, 3. A questionnaire filled out by the applicant's personal physician, 4. An evaluation (i.e. interview, physical exam and, if considered necessary, a "mini mental" exam) and 5. An overnight stay without the presence of family to test for the signs of potential incompatibility with the CCRC manner of living.

In addition, Dr. Yount the Ponds Medical Director, checked the "grapevine" of information available to him through CCRC membership associations to uncover those individuals who had already been rejected by one or more institutions. As a final precaution, if the medical risk seemed too high for an entering resident, the Ponds tacked on a $1,500 per month surcharge.

It was plain to me at this juncture that Ponds management didn't want to be "fooled" into accepting residents who would, sooner rather than later, require serious medical attention (or removal from the facility) resulting from such things as undetected dementia, alcoholism or other afflictions requiring intensive care. Alzheimers Disease, considered the worst case scenerio, was referred to here as "a poker game" because it is extremely hard to detect in its early stages.

As a rule of thumb, the management was looking for residents who were able to live at least a year in the independent residence units before being committed to the total care facility, which is much costlier to operate. One of the M.D./Medical Directors present called the "yo-yo" effect - a resident's bouncing back and forth between the nursing facility and his or her independent residence, thus occupying two "inventory" units simultaneously – his most severe problem.

Dr. Yount told me that he used to try to return residents to their apartments as quickly as possible, but that now he sought either their permanent move to the total care unit or the assurance that the medical problem was a short term one. The other side of this particular dilemma for the Ponds, was keeping an optimum level of occupancy of the total care nursing beds. If there were too many unfilled beds, the facility lost potential income, whereas if there were too many filled beds management risked not being able to honor resident contracts which guaranteed space to all Ponders when needed.

To lower vacancies, nursing beds were "rented" out to non-residents. I never learned their strategy for potentially over booking the accomodations, but Dr. Yount told me that he always wants to have 5 or 6 open beds available to Ponds residents at any given time.

By the end of the second week or so in the company of the administration group, I felt that it was in my best interests to stop "hanging out" with management types. I began to worry that I might be risking a *de facto* confirmation of residents' espionage theory concerning my presence at the Ponds...It was time to return to the natives.

I elected to conduct my ethnographic studies of the Ponds community through a mix of open-ended interviews in residents' apartments, participation in Ponds social, cultural and recreational activities and archival or library research (using the facility's own collection of historical and procedural documents as well as its medical records). My idea of getting some sort of standard questionaire to all residents was not generally well received by either Linda Copely, who was then head of the residents committee, or by Jim, because they felt that it might be interpreted by some as an invasion of privacy.

I also considered compiling a limited number of "life histories" of seemingly "typical" Ponds residents with the notion of getting another perspective on the "insiders view of the culture". Although this can be an extremely rewarding approach for the anthropologist trying to understand a culture, I reluctantly decided against it given the "total submersion" these interactions require of the researcher. The technique simply didn't fit the constraints of the time frame I had to work within.

The Ponds maintains a collection of abbreviated resident biographies, for public perusal, in the comfortable lounge just outside the doors to the central dining room. These were a big help to me in putting names together with faces and in creating a general profile of the resident population (i.e. professional backgrounds, places of former residence, vocational and advocational interests and so on). From these I was able to compile a strictly non-random sample group of potential interviewees, representing a rough cross section of the total population. From these, I was also able to produce the demographic profile of the Ponds outlined in Chapter One.

In addition to the straight demographic statistics presented in the previous chapter, I experimented with a variety of ways of classifying the resident population into categories or "types". I was attempting to find the manner in which residents' backgrounds correlated (if in fact they did) with their attitudes toward and involvement with the community, their friendship groupings and their social adjustments to their new surroundings. Also, as the original research "problem" was defined, I wanted to determine how or even if they were socialized into the community.

My working list of classificatory variables eventually included, but was not confined to: place of former residence, socio-economic status, company and/or collegial affiliation, and former profession (occupation, career etc.). I was able to reach a level of comfort with certain of these apparent "correlations" between residents' backgrounds and circumstances and their behavior.

This ultimately led to my designation of the five resident groupings: The Original Settlers, The Village Elders, The New Turks, The True Guests and The Outliers. These categories are each addressed, more of less empirically, by means of the abbreviated resident profiles contained in Chapters Five through Nine.

Mine being largely qualitative as opposed to quantitative research, I made no effort to perform sophisticated statistical analyses (e.g. the use of truly random sampling). I would attempt to lend authority to my conclusions with the use of what some social scientists refer to as "triangulation", which is the relatively straight-forward process of utilizing several sources for verification of any given "conclusion".

For example, I might test the validity of a statement made by a resident (informant) as to his or her behavior by comparing the statement with the actual behavior, and, in turn, with how others felt that he or she behaved. In line with this, and in accordance with what I was taught makes for effective ethnography, I attempted to root out variances between what my informants actually did and what they said they did and/or what they said the "should" be doing given their circumstances.

The biographies in the front lounge (and word of mouth from fellow staff and residents) revealed a very interesting and accomplished resident population. In addition to the bevy of successful attorneys, highest level corporate executives and prominent educators which I expected to find, there were a number of residents with near celebrity status, including: a New Jersey Supreme Court Justice, the nearly forgotten ex-wife of a preeminent New York real estate magnate, the lifelong agent of one of the nation's most esteemed playwrights, the CEO of a premier Ivy League college publisher, and the scientist who proposed the existence of "black holes" while working with Albert Einstein at Princeton University.

Many of the women in the group referred to in Chapter One as "non-occupational" were still quite active with the local committees and politics as well as with broader issues facing the elderly at large. I noted that The League of Women Voters was particularly well represented among this "subset" of women who were generally concerned with the welfare of society at large.

A number these ladies had advanced degrees in teaching and social work and could easily hold their own with the Ponds social services and nursing staff. In fact, there was a certain amount of resentment on the part of Ponds staffers toward these resident women - who they sometimes referred to as "ladies of leisure" - because they were perceived as "haughty", and they were thought to be "meddling" in staff matters which were none of their business.

I began working on a sort of master plan for achieving my overall research objectives. I decided to develop a list of the specific residents I wished to interview. The sample informant group would, ideally, be representative of the community at large, but would also include an equal number from each of the five categories mentioned above.

The basic background information provided by the resident biographies was helpful, as already mentioned, in terms of assuring a balanced group vis-a-vis such variables as previous residency and former profession. And the community's own archival materials (committee reports, the resident newspaper, bulletin board announcements, medical records and so on) were a big help in determining who was who.

But, additionally, I planned to ascertain whether or not the five categories I had chosen for Ponds residents where valid ones in residents' eyes. Then I would attempt to assure that my choices of representatives for each of these five categories – based upon my conclusions as an outsider - were also the likely choices of the residents themselves. I would be looking for the affirmation of my selections from Ponds staff members, from my own interactions with residents, and from my observations of residents' behavior toward and conversations with (and about) their fellow residents.

Once I had my list together, I scheduled at least one interview each day in the place most comfortable for the person being interviewed. More often than not, this turned out to be the individual's residence, which was serendipitous in that it provided insights for me into what was important to them as individuals when in the privacy of their own homes (e.g. what material possessions they had chosen to retain from much larger former residences, what their hobbies were, what they liked to read, what they had achieved in former lives, what their families were like and so on). Interviews were loosely-structured and open-ended, my thought being that I didn't want to miss anything of potential interest by confining myself to a specific list of questions.

I wanted each interview to generate for me more questions and more topics for further study, and I was willing to sacrifice a certain amount of consistency of subject matter across the interviewee group in return for a more in-depth research product. The interviews were also my primary source for networking or resourcing other interviewees.

The large majority of these individuals wanted me to have more, truly substantive information about the Ponds and its residents; they were academics and professionals in their own right and they wanted the job done well. Their interest seemed to lay in my coming away with an accurate representation of what they were about as individuals and what they represented, collectively, as a community.

In theory, good ethnography requires "blending" into the population being studied, because the mission of the ethnographer, regardless of the stated research "problem", is to figure out who the subjects think they are, and to see their world and their role in that world from their perspectives. When acceptance by the informant group has been achieved, the researcher has, theoretically, eliminated or at least greatly reduced the inclination of the informants to act differently in his or her presence (i.e. the "reflexivity" problem).

In the best case scenerio, these now accepting "natives" then continue to act "normally", indicating that the researcher has been accepted by them as one of their own. Although this ideal state probably never occurs in the real world, there are established field work techniques utilized by anthropologists and other social scientists which help to approach that goal. All of these generally involve efforts to think like the informant thinks and act like the informant acts through living the way she does.

Participant observation, which is the real backbone of enthnographic study, was my primary methodology at the Ponds. I set out to both participate in (with the objective of experiencing the place from the points of its residents), carefully observe, and document the full range of activities taking place within the Ponds Community.

31

With this in mind, I put myself on the same daily schedule as the Ponds citizenry and actively took part in early morning walks around the premises, meals with both residents and staff, staff and resident meetings, recreational activities, learning seminars, Bible groups, private and community social gatherings, visits to the health clinic, swimming, relaxing in the library and the lounges; the whole life style.

"How the Day Goes"

I set my alarm for 6:15 each morning so that I could do a two mile walk through Hightown and around the outside grounds of the Ponds. This was more than just exercise for me. The Ponds had a modest group of residents who were up and dressed and involved with various activities very early each morning. They seemed to revel in the calmness of the place before administrative types and caregivers and other service providers began to arrive and before the days scheduled activities began. I met the same individuals doing their constitutionals each morning.

For example, Henry Coulter - the 85 year old former head of research and development for a Fortune 500 electronics corporation - rode an old, bright red Schwin bicycle back and forth between the main and the service gates each morning, a distance of about one half mile each way. Another resident commented to me about this, jokingly I think, "… Merin [Mrs. Coulter] probably bought that for him so she could watch him fall off it."

Mr. Coulter was taken by the local flora and fauna, particularly the fauna. He told me that he was excited about the return of the bluebirds which had regularly inhabited the grounds until a couple of years ago when they had suddenly disappeared; he was positive that this was the year they would find their way back to the Ponds. He sometimes rambled on about Lyme disease and "chiggers" and the deer trails in the woods and the fawn he nursed back to health. He

32

and others were closely tracking the progress of the 7 young cygnets living on Heron Pond.

Mr. Coulter told me that he had been a scoutmaster for the Boy Scouts of America for many years and had spent a lot of his free time meandering among New Jersey's Pine Barrens and the woods along the Delaware River. Nature, not reminiscence about his days as a corporate research magnate, was Mr. Coulter's thing. I found that interest in nature was not at all uncommon among Ponds residents, even though most had formerly lived in and around urban centers, not in the wilds.

Les Scholten and Dr. Aresley Wayans were always in the library by 7:00 each morning because that was when the New York Times and the Wall Street Journal were delivered. Mr. Scholten, a lanky, good-natured soul, is an old time journalist to his bones, and loves to talk about his experiences, particularly those involving coverage of the FDR and Truman presidential campaigns.

He told me that on one occasion he and Robert Trout had been kept waiting for about 10 minutes beyond the scheduled start of a radio broadcast of a Truman speech to be given from the back platform of the train the President had been touring the country on.

> "Suddenly Trout and I were summoned by name on the loud speaker system to report 'immediately' to the President's car. When we arrived, Truman was laughing like hell, and he told us, 'I wanted to see how long you could ad lib' ".

Mr. Scholten had lost his wife of many years only about a month before I first met him. In spite of this, he was very excited about my research and offered many "tips" to me concerning who to talk to and about what, and about the potentially hot topics (or "scoops" as he would say)

33

developing within the Ponds community. Mr. Scholten became a real friend and a true informant in more ways than one.

Dr. Wayans initially seemed considerably more reserved than Mr. Scholten. In fact, when I first met him, I had him pegged as either a conservative Presbyterian minister from the "old school", or as the Head Master of a New England College preparatory school. He was a tall, lean man with a carefully regimented crop of white hair and small wire rim glasses which, along with his tweed sports jackets, neatly striped ties and white button down shirts, gave him a stern, sort of "Calvinistic" look.

It turned out I was wrong on both the occupation and the personality beneath the persona. Dr. Wayans was the retired chief patent attorney for a huge corporation with its roots in food processing; his "Dr." title came from his Ph.D. degree in Chemistry. Under his rather rigid exterior, he was quite amiable toward me - once he was convinced of the validity of my research - and he has a wonderful sense of (very dry) humor.

Dr. Wayans was one of the original residents of the community. He came to the Ponds at the relatively young age of 77 as the result of his wife suffering a serious fall in their home, and he strongly believes that elderly persons should not wait for this kind of mishap to precipitate their decision to enter a total care facility. He was, in addition to being the head of the resident's Health Care Committee (which had been formed to address the perceived need for an intermediate care facility), quite interested in everything administrative and procedural at the Ponds and was well informed about its history.

I found Dr. Wayans to be a reliable source of information about a lot of different things concerning the community, and he seemed to be interested in providing information for me which he felt might be helpful with my research.

All sorts of activities are in progress at the Ponds during the morning hours between breakfast and lunch. There are the bocce players, there are card and board games in progress in the various lounge areas and there are those involved with the duties of membership in one or more of the 27 Ponds residents committees.

There are shuffleboard courts (although I can't remember seeing anyone using them) and a horseshoe area which is well on its way to being totally reclaimed by nature). "Soft" aerobics classes meet several mornings a week in the large auditorium off of the quad, and there was almost always a group in the crafts shop creating water color paintings, or greeting cards, or Christmas tree ornaments, or glazed pottery.

Items from the crafts shop are put out for sale during periodical in-house craft shows, as a means for providing a little extra income for some of the residents who need it; they are also displayed in glass cases along the corridors off of the main quadrangle. In addition to the crafts shop, there is a professionally equipped woodworking shop out near the maintenance shed and the main greenhouse. This facility is heavily utilized by a small but dedicated group of woodworkers.

The group included Carl Saunders, who had just taken over as head of the resident Forum Committee, and a man who I was told by Mr. Saunders, was an accomplished furniture maker. It also included Samuel Taft who is a retired scientist of some renown and who, in addition to making shaker furniture from kits, was working on a mechanism to measure the speed of golf club swings.

The activities schedule is posted each day on the bulletin board next to the dining room entrance; typical entries might include: "10:30: Dress Sale in the Meeting Room" or "1:30: Irwin School Choir in the Main Hall" or "2:00: Food Committee meeting in the West Lounge". Additionally, one of the Hightown banks sets up for business two mornings each week in a small alcove near the reception area. During these morning hours residents also schedule hair and manicure appointments at the Ponds beauty parlor or doctors appointments in the Health Care Center. But the most prestigious of all activities here is croquet, well played.

For a small group that considers itself the elite of the resident practitioners of the sport, croquet is a very serious matter. For these individuals the game must be "English" Croquet (a.k.a. "six wicket" or "Wimbledon"), nothing else is acceptable. And there are rules governing every conceivable situation likely (or not) to arise during play. For example, one should never press the mallet into the green because this "dents" the playing surface, and a swing and a miss count as a turn (no practice swings, thank you) and, in order to "count", the ball must be far enough through the wicket so that sliding the mallet between the ball and the wicket doesn't move the ball.

Those residents who "officially" represent the Ponds in team play against other CCRC's practice almost every day. The Ponds is equipped with a large indoor croquet court, with 10 seats for spectators, which is used for practice and for tournaments during the winter months and in inclement weather. This room also has 6 stationary exercise bicycles, a rowing machine and a ping pong table. The serious croquet players at the Ponds seem to have only a barely concealed tolerance for those of lesser talent who from time to time venture to play for purely recreational purposes.

Still for the majority of participants, the daily croquet matches foster only a friendly intramural competition among the regular players, which follows them off court in the form of a sort of camaraderie among fellow aficionados. Mrs. Harvey, who had been playing religiously for almost 50 years told me that,

> "...most residents aren't really fanatical about the competition because they have their own little social croquet groups and prefer those to the stress of the competition and the interaction with people they don't know as well".

The croquet court serves as an important focal point for social interaction among the group's members, and it provides them with a means for the exchange of news about the community and its residents. I was invited as a fourth on several occasions when "regulars" weren't available.

On one such occasion, my partner was Dr. Navaro (a retired psychotherapist) who is very, very picky about how one handles one's self during a match. I am a mediocre player at best, but I was fortunate in that the good doctor is such an expert player that she managed to compensate for my bungling. We were able to narrowly avoid embarrassment (we pulled it off in overtime, and I actually made 3 of the 7 points scored!).

There was also a very small group of residents (4-6) who enjoyed lawn bowling or bocce. In fact, the total number of individuals interested in that sport was so small that it was often a problem for them to reach the critical mass of players (4) necessary for a match. And despite their efforts, they couldn't arouse enough interest within the resident body to precipitate a group large enough for inter-CCRC or even intramural bocce competition.

They did seem to have fun, though, and they weren't anywhere near as intense about the play as a number of the croquet players were. The court is located about 100 yards from the residence units in a quiet grove of huge old shade trees. It is one of the most pleasant places on campus to be during the dog days of summer.

Another nice, cool place to be on a hot summer day is the resident flower gardens. The gardens are situated on the banks of the stream flowing from the marshes on the south side of the property into Skunk Pond, the facility's largest lake. They are surrounded by another grove of old growth shade trees interspersed with winding broken slate paths.

The flowers, individual groups of which are identified with neatly- printed labels, are grown either from seeds planted in the spring or from seedlings nurtured under artificial plant lighting in the main greenhouse during the winter months. These outdoor gardens are carefully tended by the proud ladies of the residents' Garden Committee, headed by Carol Lovins.

The Ponds grows most of its own indoor and outdoor flowers and plants through the joint efforts of the resident Greenhouse committee and Jack's crew of staff grounds-keepers. And there is the rub.

Jack feels that because he is the person who is ultimately accountable for the maintenance of the grounds, including the greenhouse and including the watering of the potted plants, he should be the one who dictates how the greenhouse space is utilized. Not so according to Hal Roth - an ex-investment banker and a man of commanding authority - who spends hours each day tending to his seedlings in an area of the greenhouse allocated by Ponds management for use by the residents' Greenhouse Committee of which he is the head.

The way Mr. Roth sees it, Jack and his grounds crew actually work for him, as a resident, because, in the final analysis, he and his resident cohorts pay the salaries of all of the Ponds staff. The friction arises when Mr. Roth takes over space for which Jack's people had planned other uses or when he requisitions supplies which are not in the Ponds annual grounds budget. Due to this, Jim is routinely forced to arbitrate what he considers to be entirely "unnecessary and inappropriate" disputes between the two parties. He commented to me on several occasions that he felt Mr. Roth to be, "… an arrogant 'troublemaker' who thinks he is still a corporate CEO."

The Bible class group meets twice a week in the crafts room off of the quad. I was recruited into the group by Harold Singer, who is a retired "telephone company" (a.k.a. AT&T) man and the resident expert on the large trees blanketing the facility's grounds. Les Scholten, and Mr. and Mrs. Coulter were also in attendance, so I was not alone among strangers. Suzanne Reasner, who leads these meetings, is a young, Presbyterian minister who is also a degreed Bible scholar. She is a very outgoing person with a quick wit (perky I would say) who is surprisingly liberal in her views about such matters as her church's controversial acceptance of homosexuals into its clergy.

On the several occasions I attended, Ms. Reasner kept things moving with lively discussions about the Mediterranean travels of St. Paul. Discussions were largely secular and academic in tone. Participants, a number of whom were accomplished amateur Bible scholars themselves, were informed about the topics and obviously interested in the sessions. They seemed to have fun putting this "youngster" Suzanne to the test and sort of "strutting their stuff" for the others. I enjoyed these meetings and I came away much better informed about selected elements of the New Testament.

The Ponds operates a shuttle bus service offering regular runs to the nearby shopping malls and to downtown Hightown. This service was also available on a limited, sign-up basis for residents' individual needs such as off-premises doctors appointments, church services and so on. Even with all of these activities, however, I noted that only about 40 to 50 residents (12-14%) were in evidence outside of their apartments on any given morning. Where were the other 280 of so?

One of the more active residents told me that the number of individuals signed up for activities at any point greatly exceeded the number actually participating in the activities. I never resolved this mystery, but my educated guess would be that many were enjoying the absence of activity, and that their level of socialization with community members was, as with the extent of their living space, being downsized.

At lunch (12:30 every day), as with breakfast in the main dining hall (dining "room" doesn't do it justice), one has the option of choosing between table service or a self serve buffet; most residents choose the latter. The dining hall is an almost auditorium size room with floor to ceiling windows overlooking a large flagstone patio next to the main lake; there is a profusion of trees and flowering bushes outside the oversize windows during the warmer months. In the center of the room - which is furnished with enough tables to accommodate the entire 300 + resident body plus their guests when necessary - there is a long buffet table which is usually decorated with fresh flowers.

When set for meals, tables have linen table clothes and china (or china-like) place settings; the room has a distinctly non-institutional ambiance to it which is what residents have come to expect. The Ponds offers a relatively wide variety of mainly American style cuisine. Meals are not fancy, but they are well balanced; portions are generally small and seasoning, especially salt, is used sparsely.

Both Jim and the Ponds head chef know that they can count of a visit from Mrs. Kirkland, head of the resident's food

40

committee, if either quality or service fall below the minimum standards acceptable to her as a former society hostess of some renown and the author of one of the standards of gracious entertaining.

Typical luncheon fare will include one or more soups, a variety of cold salads, assorted cold cuts for sandwiches, a choice of beverages (which are served by waitresses after people are seated) and several deserts, always including fresh fruits. Residents are involved in animated discussions - about the morning's activities, about somebody they haven't seen in a while, about a new book someone has read and so on – while waiting their turns to serve themselves in the lines on either side of the center buffet.

After eating, some residents linger in twos and threes in the foyer outside the dining hall to briefly discuss afternoon activities, dinner plans etc. before returning to their residences to rest, or catch up on correspondence, or sun themselves on their patios. There is virtually no activity in any of the common areas between about one o'clock and three thirty or so.

There were two resident-initiated efforts to break these afternoon lulls during my stay, however. One of these was the "Ponds Ponders" debacle. Joyce Sandler, who, as the newest member of the resident library committee, was in charge of the stocking of the outlying resident lounges with reading materials. She had earned her Ph.D. from Yale in the late 1940's in the field of American literature, and was a preeminent expert on the lives and works of Robert and Elizabeth Browning. It was her feeling that because of the extraordinary collection of professional talent within the Ponds community, there would still remain a hunger within the group to keep on learning.

With this in mind, Mrs. Sandler and Rosalie Gardiner organized what they called the "Ponds Ponders" sessions.

The idea was that residents who had achieved a certain level of eminence within their respective professions would give talks to the other interested residents, with a question and answer session at the end. Mrs. Sandler was to kick the whole thing off with a lecture and discussion about the "dramatic monologue" form of poetry construction, which was revolutionized by the Brownings.

The Ponds Ponders idea was one that seemed to me, intuitively, to be a good one. But it wasn't. One would think, logically, that some of these very accomplished individuals, particularly those who were former educators, would be thrilled with the idea of imparting their wisdom to others. One might also think that individuals accomplished in their own right would enjoy learning from others like themselves. Apparently not so. Mrs. Sandler had very little luck finding volunteers to give talks. She managed one more (which I was unable to attend) by the scientist who discovered the first "black hole" in the universe, but then things dried up. The limited attention span of the audience was a major problem. It was nap time for many and they just couldn't beat their biorhythms.

But what was a real surprise to me was that most of the residents were no longer truly interested in discussing their former professions. In a large sense, they had "been there, done that" and they were ready to move on with their new lives in this more or less egalitarian setting populated by their professionally and socio-economically equal peers.

The other effort, sponsored by the same individuals, was the formation of a Ponds Choir group. This failed, according to Mrs. Gardiner, because, "… nobody had the energy to attend practices."

The swimming pool is open between 10:00 am and noon each morning in the summer and between 3:00 and 4:30 each afternoon, when a local Red Cross certified teenager named

42

Jennifer was on duty as a lifeguard. There was a small group of dedicated swimmers who convened in and around the pool each afternoon before "cocktail hour". Some, who were there for the sun and a quiet read, just dunked themselves from time to time to cool off. Others who were more serious about their exercise, however, had established rigorous regimens of lap swimming.

At least several of these "regulars" had known each other (or had had mutual acquaintances) as friends and/or neighbors for many years before coming to the Ponds. The swimmers gathered their towels and other paraphernalia and headed back to their apartments when Jennifer announced the closing of the pool and prepared to padlock the wrought iron entrance gate.

Swimming is my exercise of choice also, so I was a regular at the pool and I got to know some in the group quite well (unfortunately some too didn't warm up to me; they seemed uncomfortable with their notion that I was "studying" them). Flow Mortenson, the widow of a prominent professor of sociology at one of the Ivies, however, was quite interested in my project. As the wife of someone who had traveled widely and produced extensive ethnographic analyses, she said that she empathized with me concerning the difficulties she knew I was to encounter trying to blend in with the natives.

She took it upon herself to provide for me the names and bios (and foibles and politics and alliances and misconceptions etc.) of some of those who she considered to be the community's key "players". Mrs. Mortenson also cautioned me that, "…you shouldn't put yourself in a CCRC until you are 80."

Dinner at the Ponds is at 6:00 p.m. There is no alcohol either served or allowed in the facility's dining hall during regularly scheduled meals. There were pre-dinner cocktail

43

parties in the private residences virtually every day, however. These almost always began at 5:00 and rarely, I was told, involved more than about eight people including the host(s). There was more than one cocktail "circuit" at the Ponds during my stay there. Circuit membership roughly corresponded to the membership of the social cliques within the community. These gatherings, I found out from personal experience, also served as the means for the informal interrogation of newcomers to the community, like me.

At these soirees the conversation was animated and non-controversial for the most part. I heard a few complaints about such things as neighbors' televisions played too loud or too late and appliances not repaired properly, but most of the talk was about the enjoyment of life at the Ponds. I am not sure how my presence influenced the mood or the subject matter of the conversations, but I did generally receive a friendly, albeit thorough, grilling about my own background and about the findings of my studies of the community.

Members of a given cocktail circuit would rotate the hosting of these small affairs, which were arranged two or more weeks in advance. Attendees would have reserved a table for themselves in the dining hall in order to extend the social event through the dinner hour. Those not included in a cocktail circuit sometimes referred to those who were as the "cocktail crowd", and the revelers were perceived by the non-participants (with a certain amount of envy it seemed to me) as being somewhat flamboyant in character. Mrs. Copley, former head of the residents' Forum Committee, and her husband (a Princeton real estate executive) hosted the first of these parties that I attended.

At this party, in addition to Mr. and Mrs. Copley, the group included an inveterate world traveler with a Ph.D. in Spanish literature, a chemical engineer, and a prominent New Jersey Supreme Court Justice and his wife. Mrs. Copley told me that she believed that the short one hour duration of these get-togethers was the *de facto* means for limiting the alcohol intake of the participants; a sort of unspoken form of social control. The hosts stopped serving drinks in time for the group to get itself to the dining room just after the other residents had settled in and begun to place their orders.

Dinners at the Ponds were relatively formal, somewhat ritualized events which seemed to call for a certain decorum. Gentlemen were expected to wear sport jackets and ties, and, in line with Emily Post protocol of old, white shirts were always expected after 6:00 p.m. As with the typical upscale, WASP golf or country club set, however, sports jackets could and would be any color of the rainbow – the more eye popping the better – and fabric patterns often looked as if they had been fashioned from Laura Ashley curtains. Women generally sported cocktail attire whether or not they had in fact attended a pre-dinner cocktail party (and even through there were no cocktails permitted in the dining hall itself).

There were always fifteen minutes or so of friendly socializing in the large fourier in front of the dining room entrance, where residents arrived on foot, in wheel chairs and in the controversial electric carts. By New Jersey State law, wheel chairs must be permitted in the dining room, but the Ponds own protocol required residents to transfer from their wheelchairs to the standard dining room chairs once inside. And the electric carts were parked by a teenager - hired by the Ponds for that specific purpose - in the main auditorium across the quad.

Certain residents always headed for the same spots while waiting for the two large doors of the dining room to swing open. Dr. Wayans, for example, was invariably seated on the recessed chair with the high arch on the left side of the dining room doorway. He told me, with that dry humor of his, "…this is the coffin chair." and a nearby female resident, who had obviously overheard the good doctor's description, commented to her companion, "...it looks like a sarcophagus." Others staked out claims to specific spots on the padded benches surrounding the indoor plantings in the center of the quad, or a chair at the small corner table or a couch near the entrance to the library.

When the doors to the dining room swung open, the quad emptied almost immediately. Everyone seemed to know exactly where they were going to sit and with whom, and the whole seating process – for everyone except the cocktail crowd - was completed very quickly. I found that seating arrangements for meals were extremely important to Ponders; some even became disoriented when others changed their "regular" seating. Then came the cocktail crowd.

Whether it was planned that way or not, I noted that it was typical for this crowd to make its entrance after the other Ponds residents were already seated. In fact their entrance each evening was sometimes referred to as their "grand entrance" by those not involved, due to the fact that the partygoers were sort of "showcased" as they sauntered casually through the center of the dining room chatting happily and maybe somewhat boisterously with each other.

Waitresses served all diners at their tables.

The food was generally good, and all of the major food groups were well represented. Sal Trematossi, Ponds head chef, with the input of the resident food committee chairwoman, Melanie Kirk, made an effort to both select (and describe) each day's menu with a certain continental flourish which added to the "elegance" of the dining experience. Typically, one was able to choose among several appetizers (e.g. a shrimp cocktail, a liver pate, a house salad) or a soup de jour, several entrees (normally including a chicken dish and a seafood dish) and several desserts (there was always *Jell-O* in one form or another in there somewhere).

And there were some unique but very practical rules of dining etiquette. For example, flowers were removed from table tops and placed on the floor next to the table so that diners could see each other while talking, and one's Menu was placed upright on the table when one was ready to order, and one ordered all three courses at the same time. One evening I asked Mrs. Copley about the boisterous party going on at one of the tables near ours. She informed me that it was only one of the several resident social "divas", Sarah Jenson, "holding court" with this evening's representatives of her extensive friendship group; a nightly occurrence she told me.

All of this style and fanfare resulted in a sort of a refined (leaning toward the efficient rather than the stuffy) but carefree ambiance surrounding the dining experience for many of the residents, possibly reminiscent of their social gatherings in their former suburban communities.

For the majority, the day (at least the part of the day that involved community socializing) ended shortly after dinner. Although there were movies shown in one of the lounges (actually videos played on a 50+ inch television set) several nights a week (e.g. "Mr. Smith Goes to Washington", "Mr. Deeds Goes to Town", "Casablanca" or "Three Coins in a Fountain"), they were sparsely attended.

Dr. Wayans told me that he wanted to be finished with dinner in time to see the PBS News on his own television, and speedy returns to residences seemed to be the norm for most of the group. As previously mentioned, many of these residents were up at the crack of dawn each morning, so after dinner socializing was kept to a bare minimum.

Chapter Three

Politics, Issues & Budgets
And Committees and More Committees

The Ponds community, viewed functionally, breaks down into three groups: administration, floor staff and residents. "Administration" includes the department heads and their immediate clerical and supervisory help (the Director's Office, Accounting, Marketing, Resident & Social Services, Medical and Grounds & Maintenance).

The "floor" staff, as the term is used here, consists of the RN's, LPN's, nurses aids and companions; those in direct personal and/or "hands on" contact with residents on a day to day basis. As with any segmented community, there are frictions at the Ponds resulting from varying factional objectives, perceived differences in status, imperfect information, lack of communication and so on.

As was already mentioned, many Ponders were unhappy with their lack of representation on the Ponds Board of Directors. They were suspicious that revenues from the Ponds - the premier institution in the Christian Homes group of elder care facilities in terms of both status and profitability - were being diverted to the other members of the group. This, they felt, was the reason that certain improvements (e.g. intermediate care hospice units and a third physician) were not forthcoming in spite of steadily increasing resident fees.

Residents, some of whom were formerly senior level business executives, reviewed the Christian Homes financial statements each year to measure - as best they could given the lack of operating unit detail - the economic health of the place and to assure themselves that their fees were being spent wisely.

48

At one point several years after the inception of the Ponds, a resident by the name of Overton mistook payments made by the Ponds on a note held by the parent corporation, Christian Homes of New Jersey, as a diversion of Ponds residents' fees for use by the other homes within the group. After filing a suite against CHNJ, he was proven incorrect in his assumptions and asked to leave. His allegations, however, turned out to be the genesis of future resident suspicions as to the "incorrect" use of Ponds residents' fees.

Jim, as Ponds' Director, took the "official" position that residents' fees from any one of the homes in the group were eligible for use anywhere within the group. Mr. Overton told residents, however, that their fees, with the exception of a contribution to corporate overhead, were almost never used for the well being of the Ponds itself. The truth may never be known outside of corporate headquarters - because financial statements don't break out expenses by operating unit - but many residents felt that with a board seat they could demand access to the records documenting the use of their fees.

Another source of friction between the Ponds administration and the residents was the absence of a third resident physician. There had been three full time resident physicians at the facility up until about a year before my arrival. At that time, one of the three physicians, a lady doctor who was immensely popular with the residents, was transferred to Monte Vista, one of the other CHNJ facilities which was in the initial stages of staffing up its medical department.

Ponds residents were promised that the third physician slot would remain open only for as long as it took to find a new doctor. There was no time frame promised for the replacement, however, and that was the rub. The administration assured residents that the job was budgeted, but residents complained that there didn't seem to be any recruitment effort going on.

Many Ponders, however, felt (rightly so as it turns out) that Jim, at the behest of CHJN corporate, was playing a sort of waiting game in order to save money, and that maybe they would be forced to make do with two rather than three physicians. The two remaining Ponds doctors, Coburn and Yount, would admit to being occasionally over worked (or under staffed as the case may be), but they were aware of the politics surrounding the issue, and would not openly advocate either for or against the replacement of their former colleague.

And Jim, in spite of his "official" position vis-à-vis the residents, told me that he didn't feel that the "volume" warranted a third physician. He also confirmed that he had been asked by corporate to "go slow" on the rehire due to "budget constraints".

Another issue at the Ponds was the absence of a true intermediate care unit for those who required help with bathing, dressing, medication etc., but who were not yet ready for total nursing care. It was both state and Ponds policy that nobody without state certification as a medical aid could render any assistance to residents involving hands on contact. Most of the companions hired privately by residents were not certified medical aids, so all residents' needs for hands on assistance had to be provided by a mobile assisted care team (as discussed in Chapter One).

This team was made up of an RN and a nurse's aid (Nina Boyer and Cindy Rogers, respectively) and a Practical Nurse (Betsy Kleine) who reported to one of the Ponds two head nurses, Catelin Craig. This group, which scheduled regular appointments with residents for specific assistance needs, navigated the hallways by means of a modified electric golf cart. Residents felt this to be an inefficient, makeshift way of handling their needs for intermediate care.

Although Jim pointed out that very few CCRC's offered dedicated intermediate care units, CHNJ had commissioned a study to determine the feasibility of a facility which would include live-in residences for those requiring this level of care; the project was known locally as "Building 50". Dr. Wayans was also the head of the Building 50 Committee. In addition to the budget considerations involved with an undertaking of this size, there was the practical problem of sewerage treatment that had to be dealt with.

As it turned out, the Ponds would have to draw on the sewerage treatment facilities of both Hightown and South Weymouth for Building 50 (the new facility would straddle the jurisdictional boundary between the two). And both towns were in the process of petitioning the state of New Jersey for the expansion of their treatment plants. So, although there seemed to be a willingness on the part of CHNJ to go ahead with the project, it wasn't going to happen within the time frame envisioned by concerned residents.

A related issue was that of hospice care for the terminally ill. Jeanne Sandler, the resident Brownian expert who was testing the "Ponds Ponders" concept, was the first of the residents to bring this need to my attention. She felt that those who were living out their final days in the nursing facility, some without visits from friends or family, deserved, if not a full fledged hospice unit, at least some ministerial attention from former friends still residing in the independent living units.

Several other residents voiced this same concern to me, and Jim told me that he had heard word that there was a resident hospice committee being formed. Jim also told me, however, that a formal hospice unit was virtually out of the question due to the high costs of staffing such a unit 24 hours a day, seven days a week.

Both from my personal observations and from numerous conversations with Ponds staff, I concluded that residents entering the nursing facility on a permanent basis were almost totally ignored by those remaining in the residence units, even some of their former "friends". Whatever the reasons for this (one thought which crossed my mind was that those fortunate enough not to require full time nursing care may have been denying their own vulnerability to it), individuals in the Ponds nursing care facility were perceived by the majority of the other residents as virtual "non-residents".

Because the intermediate care team was stretched to its limits with the heavy demands placed upon it, Ponds administration was looking at various ways to meet the assisted care needs of the residents – with no incremental costs to it - while awaiting resolution of the Building 50 project. Jim intended to make it a requirement that residents' companions obtain state certification as nurse's aids and go on the Ponds payroll. Their services – many of which were currently being handled by Nurse Craig's team - would then be billed back to residents on an "as used" basis, thus, theoretically costing the Ponds nothing.

These new arrangements would involve major organizational changes in the Ponds floor staff, and they had the potential of causing serious friction between and among floor staff, administration, residents and private contractors.

Many of the companions had become attached to their employers and vice versa, and companions were afraid of losing their jobs. Most seemed to enjoy their current status as free agents and independent contractors (for a variety of reasons), and were not interested in staff positions. The situation was a complex one.

Private companions felt that they were currently better compensated than they would be as Ponds employees because they believed that the Ponds had to pay them less than they charged the residents in order to make a profit on their services. And there was the whole matter of health care benefits. Some companions felt that the Ponds would assign them just enough hours to avoid the full time employee designation, thus not having to pay medical benefits.

The health care benefits issue had finally come to a head, and the Ponds administration scheduled a series of three informational/ fact-finding meetings with the private companions as a group. I attended the second of these meetings, the purpose of which was to ascertain the concerns of the companion group and to present management's initial position.

The meeting was also attended by several of the residents who were concerned about the future status of their companions. The administration team included, in addition to Jim, Debbie Dempsy-O'Brien (the CHNJ Vice President in charge of labor relations), Katie Bee (Ponds' Admissions/Marketing Coordinator) and Ponds Controller, Maggie Lane.

Jim kicked off the meeting by introducing the admin team and stating the purpose of the meeting. He assured the group that, "...management has no intention of trying to separate companion from employer." He then provided answers to several of their most pressing concerns:

> "Yes", they would need to be state certified as nurses aids if they were involved in any hands on contact with residents; "Yes", their seniority would be honored; "Yes", their certification expenses would be covered; "Yes", they could remain with their current employer; "Yes", they could follow their current employer if transferred to the nursing facility; and "Yes", they would receive medical insurance (a $500 per person "stop loss", after

which 80% of everything over the $100 deductible would be covered).

Jim continued the meeting by taking questions from the floor such as, "...can we opt to not take the insurance coverage?" (answer: "No"); "...how is seniority defined? (answer: "input is needed from the employer, but our intention is to keep you financially 'whole'"); "...how will our hours change?" (answer: "...they won't change with regard to your existing employer, but whether you get time and a half for some employment and to whom it is charged has to be worked out.")

Other questions were asked about "no frills" medical policies, coordination with a spouse's policy, coverage of dependents, who is in charge in the nursing facility (i.e. the companion or the resident nurse) and so on. Jim answered what he could (or what he was authorized to answer) and promised to get back to them with the answers to the questions he couldn't answer.

Things were going pretty well until one of the companions became somewhat more confrontational by framing her question about overtime pay with what sounded like a challenge to the administration: "Are you telling me that I have to...even though it is against my will?" She, it seems, was wary of schemes to reduce overall compensation through such ploys as converting overtime to straight time by requiring companions to put in their overtime hours working for a second resident. Debbie Dempsy-O'Brien quickly jumped in with the statement that,

> "...we cannot possibly resolve every possible variation of every theme at this meeting, and the meeting was not designed to do so...each question will be given careful consideration and policy proposals will be offered...everyone will be kept informed and asked to participate at each step."

Jim ended the meeting by saying how much he appreciated the generally "non-adversarial" manner in which it had been conducted.

Jennie Reed, who was the private companion of my next door neighbor Mrs. Cousins, was sitting next to me during the meeting. Jennie said,

> "I see some trouble spots with these changes, mainly over jurisdictional issues. For example, nurses aids in the nursing facility will never agree to perform some of the less pleasant aspects of their patient care while the personal nurses aids sit there doing nothing. There is no question in my mind that companions would get a pay cut, and that those who really needed the overtime - some work as much as 140 hours a week - would be badly hurt financially."

This issue was not resolved during my stay, but it continued to be a source of friction between the private companion group and Ponds administration and, to a lesser extent, between residents and administration.

One of Jim's personal frustrations with resident attitudes and behavior was what he saw as a lack of caring or concern for fellow residents. He was referring both to quality of life matters and to matters of community involvement. For example, it particularly bothered Jim that many residents had virtually no idea of what was going on with those living right next door to them; there didn't seem to be any feelings of "neighborhood" in the various buildings or hallway groupings.

Because the Ponds didn't have the staff to keep tabs on every resident all of the time, the staff relied upon residents to report unusual patterns of activity with their neighbors (e.g. failure to leave their apartments for extended periods of time, slovenly appearance or other deviations from patterned activity or demeanor etc.), The Ponds administration was worried that it might not be able to catch health or emotional problems in their early stages, before they evolved into crisis situations.

It turned out that management was not alone in this concern. Linda Copely, former head of the resident's Executive Forum committee mentioned to me her (and their) concern shortly after my arrival at the Ponds. She had spoken to Jim about the problem, and they had discussed the formation of resident "caring teams" in charge of various hallway sectors (this was something which had been tried, with some success apparently, at Avon, one of the other CHNJ facilities).

Jim, feeling that many Ponds residents had an "elitist" attitude toward their peers, was pessimistic about the effectiveness of this approach. He did agree, however, to pose the question to other CCRC managers during their regular consortia meetings, and he also told Mrs. Copely that he would ask his own staff for specific proposals for resolving the problem. That, though, was about as far as the addressing of this aspect of resident apathy got during my stay.

One the most controversial topics at the Ponds was the annual budget. The budget was the source of both intra administration friction (e.g. departmental rivalries for increased allocations) and administration-resident friction (e.g. residents' lack of access to the process). Ponds department heads did not look forward to the annual budgeting ritual; they knew that many of their pet projects would be knocked out of the final package and they disliked the drudgery of assembling all of the "knit-picky" details required by CHNJ corporate.

Jerry Bradford, head of Grounds and Maintenance, was upset that his people didn't have a more realistic gas allowance for business related travel which was done at the request of the administration. He also felt that he was seriously under staffed, and he resented the fact that his employees were routinely sent to help out at the other CCRC's in the CHNJ group while still being expected to finish their Ponds assignments on time.

Unlike other department heads, Jerry was asked to put his budgets together as if his department were a private corporation seeking to return 30% of its "income" (i.e. its budget allocation) to the "bottom line." To him, this was nothing more than a request to spend 30% less than he needed to get the job done. Additionally, he had a hard time "bidding out" projects - because CHNJ, which paid the bills, had the reputation of being a slow payer.

Sarah Langley, who was in charge of resident activities for the nursing care unit, gave me a rough idea of the budget building process:

> "First I assemble the cost details for my particular area of responsibility with attendant commentary on additions and subtractions from my current budget. This is then submitted to Jim and the Ponds controller, Maggie Lane. If there are questions or changes - something that has never happened to me - I would be called in to discuss these. After Jim and his staff have reached agreement on all of the departmental budgets they meet with members of the resident Financial Advisory Committee to advise them as to what would be forwarded to CHNJ corporate for its review. The last step is submission to the CHNJ Board of Directors for final approval."

It is during the corporate budget review that capital projects, staff additions and so on for all nine of the CHNJ operating units are decided upon for the upcoming fiscal year. By necessity, if major projects or staff additions (i.e. those requiring spending beyond the facility's anticipated revenues) are approved for a particular member of the nine CCRC group, others in the group must contribute their revenues and postpone their own projects in order to provide the funding for their sister facility.

Ponds residents are not involved in or informed of what goes on at this level of review. But, as has already been mentioned, the belief that their fees are being used by other CCRCs in the group is a source of irritation for a number of residents, and this perception serves as the rationale behind their push for representation on the CHNJ Board.

In response to the budget constraints he was forced to work under, Jim had strategies for both increasing revenues and reducing expenses. His plan for increasing revenues included: a.) attracting younger, theoretically healthier (hence requiring less use of the high cost nursing care facility) residents through a re-designed marketing effort, b.) developing better methods for detecting applicants with serious illness, and c.) selling incremental, personalized services to residents without increasing staff (e.g. help with bill paying, taxes etc., maintenance of small gardens next to patios etc.) or "unbundling" existing services and pricing them individually.

On the cost cutting side, Jim planned to, among a long list of other things: a.) reduce food waste by more accurately calculating the amount of Ponds food consumed by staff (i.e. many brought their lunches and breakfasts from home), b.) keep nursing beds full even if it meant marketing them to non-residents, c.) keep residence units fully occupied and "turning over", d.) add private companions to the Ponds payroll, e.) defer the hiring of a third physician (as well as any other "non-essential" employees), and f.) purchase health care for residents through a third party provider.

In addition to all of this, Jim was always looking for ways to maximize the use of existing staff by both increasing their tasks and improving their efficiency. Over the months I heard a number of complaints by floor staff, for example, about Jim "snooping around" to see who was spending too much time on coffee breaks; it was rumored that these people were asked to perform additional duties.

Another source of annoyance to certain residents and to Jim's staff was the use of the small, but quite expensive electric carts designed for those with mobility problems. Every resident seemed to have an opinion about the subject. Merin Coulter, who, though in her late 80's still drove to Florida every year in her own car, told me that she felt it was unsafe for people "their age" to be driving these carts "all over the place". Some felt that the carts presented a fire hazzard while others believed that many who drove the carts could walk "just fine" and didn't need them.

As already mentioned, Ponds administration wanted to "duck the bullet" on this issue, but was forced to take a stand. The end result was that a "law" went into effect whereby residents must have a legitimate medical need for using the carts, and that need was to be determined solely by Dr. Coburn or Dr. Yount, the resident physicians. And to further address the safety issue, the Ponds would determine where the carts could be used (e.g. not in the dining room) and would hire an attendant to provide valet parking for them during mealtimes and other events taking place in the common areas.

Committees And More Committees

Even through CHNJ had ultimate control over how the income from all of its facilities was used, resident Committees at the Ponds provided residents with some say in how the community operated and in its quality of life. As the elite members of the CHNJ group, Ponders suggestions – as

59

proposed through their committees - were respectfully considered by the administration and, when reasonable (and affordable), generally complied with.

At the time of my research there were 27 resident committees at the Ponds. These were almost equally divided between those concerned with practical and administrative matters (e.g. the Executive Forum Committee, the Financial Advisory Committee, the Grounds Committee, the Food Committee) and those concerned with social and recreational pursuits (e.g. the Library Committee, the Garden Committee, the Films Committee etc.).

By far the most important of the committees was the Executive Forum Committee, which oversaw all of the other committees, and which was the direct liaison with Ponds administration (both local and corporate). This committee was also concerned with issues affecting the welfare of the elderly at large (such as living wills). By its charter, all residents are automatically "members" of the Executive Forum Committee, which is not allowed to charge dues. The stated "mission" of the committee is to,

> "Help residents live happily at the Ponds...provide recreation and pleasure through social, cultural and religious programs, without profit making intent... [and] to represent the common interests of the residents in working with the administration."

I attended my first Executive Forum Committee meeting two weeks after I began my research. I was invited by the then committee chairwoman, Linda Copely, because I had agreed to give a short talk about my research methodology and objectives. The meetings were structured affairs following a sort of colloquial interpretation of *Robert's Rules of Order* (or the like). Mrs. Copley began this particular meeting by informing the group that,

"...due to time constraints [my talk was apparently one of these], only the most vital committees involved with matters of resident welfare will speak; others will stand up to be recognized only."

She informed the group that another new committee – Housekeeping – was being added, and then she asked her Treasurer, Arminger Wells, to give his report concerning current financial balances and the like.

The next report, a sobering one from the head of the Financial Advisory Committee, revealed that CHNJ had had an operating deficit of $559 thousand for the fiscal year just ended. Also, approximately $1.5 million of the $6.6 million Ponds fund for capital expenditures would have to be spent during the current year on state-mandated items. These included such things as a sprinkler fire system for the nursing care unit, new siding for residence apartments, new transformers and the completion of an oil spill cleanup.

When it was her turn, the inimitable Melanie Kirk, head of the Food Committee, proposed to us that,

"...food is the most controversial subject known to man or woman. And our food staff has a big job serving 1000 meals a day with seven menus."

Then Dr. Ardsley Wayans, who was chairman of the Health Care Committee (formerly the Building "50" Committee, but which was now also formulating a position on the companion issue), informed the group that studies of both the intermediate care facility blueprints and the companion issue were underway. Finally, after recognizing the heads of the other 23 committees (most of whom were not in attendance it seemed by the general lack of response), Mrs. Copely opened up the floor for questions.

It turned out that the hot topic of the evening was the hiring of the third resident physician. Dr. Wayans, who was also chairman of the resident's Physician Search Committee, told the resident body that there were,

> "...deplorable healthcare conditions resulting from the loss of our third doctor to Monte Vista...the earliest appointment I can get for a physical is August 1 [about a month away]...I see Dr. Yount here until 6:00 doing paper work, and the facility's healthcare in general is not adequate."

He assured the group, however, that his committee was,

> "... addressing the situation, making progress, and should be trusted as representing the resident's interests."

Mrs. Copely invited any having more current information (meaning Jim) to speak up, "...this being the proper forum for release of this information." At this point Jim, in a surprise move, stated that the administration was close to making an offer to a lady doctor who both they and the residents liked ("which residents?" I asked myself).

Nothing came of this during my stay, however, and the complaining continued, so I am still not sure what kind of political posturing was going on behind the corporate veil. The meeting ended with a short introduction to and talk by the newest visiting researcher, yours truly.

The Executive Forum Committee meetings were where most of the "power politics" between residents and administration took place. Meetings of the majority of individual committees were largely focused on recreational and quality of life matters, however.

The Workshop Committee, for example, was involved with the affairs of both the woodworking shop and the crafts center. This committee researched projects for the group (e.g. jewelry making, toys for grandchildren etc.), helped with the requisition of supplies, and organized the sale of the arts and crafts produced by residents.

The Sports Committee spent much of its time with the arrangements for intramural and inter-CCRC croquet competitions (naturally), but also took an interest in activities with much lower participation rates such as shuffle board, bocce, ping pong and, largely for the kids, bumper pool. A resident suggested to me that there were many more individuals registered for the Ponds "sports" activities than there were individuals actually participating in these activities; in my experience, he hit the nail right on the head.

The Health Care Committee represented a sort of *de facto* liaison between those residents who were confined to the Ponds nursing care unit (either temporarily or permanently) and those residing in the independent living units. The members of this committee organized birthday parties, wheeled in selections of library books on carts, procured necessities (e.g. shampoo, tooth paste, cosmetics etc.) for those interned, delivered mail, served tea, escorted patients to Ponds entertainment functions, and all sorts of other things. But the committee's main function - at least from the standpoint of its sequestered clients, most of whom saw family and friends only sporadically - was to provide friendly visits and a link with the outside world.

George Sizor, a former AT&T line engineer, was the head of the Grounds Committee. This seemed particularly appropriate to me, because George was totally enamoured with the profusion of beautiful old growth trees on the Ponds grounds, and he walked the property most afternoons to check on his "babies". I was his "guest" on one of these walks, following an upbeat lunch with George and Martin Stevens, the former maintenance head of a very prestigious Ivy League university. I learned more about the habits of the deciduous trees of the Northeast than I had learned as a biology major in college.

George monitored the lives of virtually all of the adult trees on the Ponds property and he was prepared to offer a guided tour to anyone interested, at "the drop of a hat" (as he and his peers were fond of saying). Anyway, the Grounds committee was in a continuous state of negotiation with Jerry Bradford and his maintenance crew with regard to the placement of new bushes, the layout of decorative plantings etc. in addition to the care of the old growth trees.

Here is a brief synopsis of what some of the other Ponds committees were up to: The House Committee was involved with the redecoration of the day rooms and other public areas. The Program Committee arranged for live entertainment for the residents (there had been 19 such events during the 12 months prior to my stay). The Play Readers Committee performed readings of plays (8 during my residency). The Book Review Committee, the Lost and Found Committee, the Films Committee, the Dial-an-Activity Committee, the Library Committee, the After Dinner Committee and the Archives Committee were committed pretty much to what their titles implied.

Some of these resident committees, as already mentioned, were considered more prestigious and politically powerful than others by the resident body at large and, in some cases, by Ponds administration. Some, such as the Library Committee, with its 47 members, grew and prospered. Others, such as the Creative Stationary Committee shrank to almost nothing, and one, the Singing Committee, actually went out of existence due to lack of attendance.

And there was the whole political side of the Ponds committee system. The committees yielding the most prestige and the highest political leverage were the Executive Forum Committee, the Financial Advisory Committee, the

Building 50 Committee and the Food Committee. These were the ones which were generally involved with the welfare of the resident population at large, and they were the ones which interacted most directly with Ponds administration.

These prestigious committees were headed largely by the segment of the resident population I refer to as "The Village Elders". The Village Elders (who are addressed in more detail in later chapters focusing on resident profiles), as the name implies, were looked to for wisdom and leadership by the other residents. They had generally been Ponds residents for longer, and they held the key positions on the key committees. They jealously guarded their authority and status.

Conversely, many of the heads of the lesser committees were held (mainly by default rather than by choice) by another group who I refer to as "The New Turks". These were newer members of the community who wanted to take activist roles in determining quality of life matters. They were, generally, highly accomplished professionals, including a significant number from the academic world.

I found that the New Turks were more interested in change, while the Village Elders tended toward the status quo. Needless to say, the two "factions" clashed from time to time (with each other and with Ponds administrators) over what each determined to be in the "best interests" of the community.

Because there were more residents interested in committee leadership than there were positions of committee leadership available, a series of "sub-committees" had evolved over time. For example, the Library Committee became segmented into the Library Committee, the Archives Committee, and the Book Reviews Committee.

The Grounds Committee had broken off into the Grounds Committee, the Garden Committee, the Greenhouse Committee and the Maintenance Committee. And so on.

At some point, Carl Saunders, the incoming chairman of the Executive Forum Committee, even created the notion of committee "counsels", thus providing more administrative slots in the resident committee structure.

In any event, the committee system was in good health during the time I was in residence. It seemed that many of these Ponders, who had been leaders within their respective fields during their professionally active years, were still interested in exercising at least some control over their current lives.

Chapter Four

Simlifying Life
and the Return to Mother Earth

I was quite interested from the outset in why my informants had chosen a CCRC as their final residence. So, even though my interviews (and casual conversations) with residents were largely open ended, I did ask everyone I spoke with how they had decided on the assisted care community as a residence type and why they had chosen the Ponds in particular. What I found was that a majority of the individuals I spoke with had lived most of their married lives in large homes in affluent suburban communities.

At some point, generally after their children had left home or their local friends had moved elsewhere, these upper middle class whites began what I have found to be a pattern of the downsizing of physical space. The process – which I also observed in subsequent research in other settings – roughly parallels the changed life circumstances of advancing age (e.g. declining mobility and/or mental acuity).

In some cases the first step in the downsizing for these Ponders was a move to a significantly smaller residence in a similar setting (e.g. a smaller house or a condominium). In other cases, the move was directly from a large house to the CCRC or its equivalent. In the latter situation, the move was often the response to an accident in the home or the impairment of the mobility of one or both partners.

These were not the only scenarios I found, but they were by far the most prevalent. I also encountered a few residents, some of whom had never been married (or who had lost a spouse much earlier in life), who had lived in apartments for extended periods of time before coming to the Ponds.

And I found a small number of others who had spent periods of time living with their children's families or who had lived in other types of non-assisted community settings. Still others had been moving from place to place over the years due to their professions etc.

But in almost every case the general direction of the moves had been from larger to smaller spaces and/or from relatively high complexity life styles to simpler ones. In this regard, one of the younger residents, Jeanne Sandler (77) told me,

> "...older [Ponds residents] keep making their worlds smaller and smaller until they are left with just their own egos, and they begin taking a possessive attitude toward such things as the community's doctors [they make statements like] ..they're taking 'my' doctor." [this in reference to the transfer of the Pond's third female physician to another CCRC in the group]."

Dr. and Amy Wayans were charter residents of the Ponds. They had moved to the facility from a comfortable seven room apartment in Queens while they were in their mid seventies (which was closer to the average age of Ponds residents at the time), not out of necessity, but because they had anticipated their future needs for assisted care living earlier than most.

They made the decision in spite of the fact that they had already built their "ideal" retirement home on a 1.5 acre mountain ridge in central New Jersey. The decision was influenced by the fact that Dr. Wayan's mother had waited until she was too sickly to qualify for admittance to a CCRC type facility.

Dr. Wayans was convinced, however, that most elderly don't consider such a move until they have experienced a serious accident in their homes. One example of that situation which

I later ran across was that of Dr. Regis Winford, a former professor of economics at Harvard, who told me that he had had no intention of giving up his large suburban home until the day his wife Nellie, who had advanced arthritis, plunged headfirst down the front staircase of their home outside Boston.

Adaptation to the reduced space at the Ponds was, according to many of the residents I spoke with about it, relatively easy, given the paths they had taken to get there. A few, such as Flow Harrison - whose husband was an acclaimed New York City surgeon who had died shortly before Mrs. Harrison's arrival at the Ponds - said she had no problem giving up most of their material possessions to make the move. These things held little meaning for her without her former spouse.

And Emmy Kolber, who had lived all over the world as the wife of a prominent journalist, had no trouble with her move to the Ponds from her comfortable New York apartment, although she missed the younger, worldly crowd she once mixed with, and she was not happy with the "...falloff of the propriety [that had been] associated with dinner dress in the old days."

Similarly, Armenger Wells, a retired senior partner of a New York City law firm, confided in me that he had moved to the Ponds directly from a very large home in suburban New Jersey. He claimed to have had "...no trouble whatsoever "with the move from eleven or twelve rooms to three rooms ("It's not difficult at all once you have made up your mind."). He chose the particular apartment that he and his wife Ollie were in because he was allowed to plant his own flower garden along the wall between the small terrace and the living room. He and Mrs. Wells were both thrilled with not having any maintenance to worry about.

Arlene Wentworth, a retired professor of Social Development in the New York University system, was, at 67, the youngest Ponds resident. She was living happily with Hal Roth, ten years or so her senior, who had retired from a very successful career on Wall Street, and who was exercising his passion for plants as the controversial head of the Resident Greenhouse Committee. Dr. Wentworth and Mr. Roth, who were already live-in companions, looked at the Ponds at the suggestion of friends, in what she calls a "pre-readiness survey" (i.e. with the intention of buying in a 3-5 year time frame).

They ended up moving less than two years later, and had been living there 13 months when I interviewed them. Dr. Wentworth had no children of her own and, because she had no intentions of burdening her nieces and nephews, she had always planned on taking care of herself in her old age. She said,

> "We moved from a 7 room home outside of New York City but had no trouble with the transition. We were extremely well organized and had all of our possessions itemized on the computer and the manner of disposition all pre-determined beginning with garage and estate sales, donations and so on. Both of us had lived in institutions before [she in the university community, he in the Navy]."

Ed and Rachael Gelby had been Ponds residents for four years when I first met them. He was still active as an independent contractor working for a firm which planned and placed office furniture for businesses (he had sold his own office furniture business in New York City a number of years previously).

The Gelbys had been planning their eventual move to a retirement community for 18 years (since he was 60) due to the problems that their own elderly parents had caused them.

70

They were determined not to burden their own children (by far the most frequent rationale I encountered for making the move).

Also, Mr. Gelby had had a bad experience driving his wife, who had broken her knee, to a hospital emergency room in a bad section of the city. The idea of her having to do the same thing for him if the situation were reversed, frightened both of them. Although they both seemed to love everything about the place from the staff to the availability of activities, they still spent two months during each summer at their cottage in the Pocanos. Rachael Gelby told me, "You have to get away. Being around all of these old people gets to you sometimes."

I found that almost all of the Ponds residents I spoke with were relieved with not having to worry about maintenance and about entertaining. The reduction of what some, such as Desmond South, referred to as "social space" was a true relief for those who had formerly lived very active and complex lives for so many years. The truth is that the transition was not a smooth one for everyone I spoke with, however.

One of the Ponds social workers told me that the sharing of the reduced space sometimes resulted in marital conflicts. And Hannah Roamer, whose husband was a permanent resident of the nursing care unit and who was terminally ill herself, told me that she missed her old home and her old friends "terribly".

Martha Harvey was of the opinion, however, that,

> "The Ponds lessens the trauma of less space [and other transitions accompanying the move to a CCRC] because you become part of a community of age and social peers with all of the luxuries and social amenities provided."

And others were perfectly willing to wander on philosophically in my company about everything from the proper timing of the move to the proper type of individual able to successfully negotiate the transition. Ellie Barns had carefully evaluated her feelings about her own move to the Ponds. She was happy to share these feelings with me, and she also provided for me some interesting observations on the adjustment process at large.

Mrs. Barns had spent five trying years prior to her admission to the Ponds nursing her husband during his terminal cancer. She said,

> "Moving was very traumatic for me in terms of leaving old friends and in terms of disposing of things due to the much more limited space. Most of them disapproved of what I was doing; I was the first of my group to do it. In my mind there is a window of opportunity for the move in terms of age. You can't be too old to expend energy, but you have to be old enough so that the sacrifices in terms of loss of former life style are offset by the necessity of the supportive environment.
>
> Those who come with negative attitudes don't last very long...I now look at old, former friends from the standpoint of whether or not they would do well at the Ponds or an equivalent CCRC. Some have no family at all, or family who don't see them, and those definitely should be here where they can have a substitute family...most people here recognize they are in the same boat and are empathetic."

Jeanne Sandler, a former Ivy League professor renowned in the academic world for her firm grasp of Brownian verse, told me that,

"I enjoy the diversity of manners in which residents choose to decorate their apartments. Some seem to save as much as possible from former homes, even though it produces crowded living quarters. I have saved very little; I want as much open space as possible."

Many of the residents' apartments that I visited really did look as if they were miniaturized versions of much larger suburban homes. Several I saw however, like Mrs. Sandler's, contained only a small number of precious items. In some apartments the furniture seemed too large for the space, or maybe there was just too much of it. In others there was only a sparse amount of the institutional-like furniture provided by the Ponds.

In any event, looking at these apartments provided for me a real sense of which material possessions were, when push came to shove, the most valuable to their respective owners. These final consolidations of physical things, symbolizing the results of the ultimate filtering out of the material baggage of former life styles, provided invaluable insight for me into the unique personalities of the individual owners. This uniqueness was further reflected in the hallways in front of the residence units. There were, for example, personalized name plaques on many apartment doors, seasonal decorations (e.g. fall leave arrangements, spring flowers) near the thresholds and colorful doormats with cheerful messages.

Another aspect of the simplified Ponds lifestyle which seemed to be almost universally liked by the residents was the ease of entertaining. As already mentioned, there were what amounted to cocktail circuits at the Ponds. Residents would invite a few friends (generally 4-6) from their particular "crowd" over for drinks before dinner, and they in turn would be invited to other member residences on other nights; and so on.

Eventually, with this system, every resident in a given social group would have both visited and entertained every other member of that group. After each cocktail party, those involved would head to the dining hall where each would sign his or her own tab. The result was that each participating resident would be able to stay in touch socially with every member of his or her group on a regular basis, with a minimum of effort. Nobody had to cook or wash dishes, and nobody had to pick up the cost of the dinners of the others in the group.

In addition to these ongoing get-togethers, residents occasionally used the Ponds facilities for larger, usually celebratory parties. The cost, of course, was added to their normal monthly fees, but the entertaining was virtually hassle free for them. Dr. Wentworth and Mr. Roth, for example, celebrated their move to the Ponds with a large party - including both their friends at the Ponds and friends from outside - in one of the day rooms. They used a contingent of the facility's kitchen and dining room staff to cater the entire affair, which included cocktails and a sit down dinner.

Life at the Ponds, as is fairly typical of the CCRC, was carefully designed to be as stress free as possible. Some chose to keep their own cars there; a parking space was assigned to each residence unit. Many, however, were no longer able to drive safely. They utilized the regular Ponds bus service into the village, to local shopping malls and, on a limited, reservation basis, for outside doctor appointments, church services and other individual needs.

Residents did not have to go off premises for routine medical care, hair appointments, manicures or their personal banking. Monthly fees included a limited amount personalized service from the intermediate care staff which was usable at the resident's discretion (e.g. help with medication, bathing, therapeutic exercise etc.), and once a week maid service. But there were other services, as well as extended use of the included services, available on a (relatively costly) carte blanche basis.

The ease of living was, as one might expect, a primary reason that most Ponds residents had chosen the CCRC lifestyle. The inconveniences caused by the mandatory downsizing of space were, according to most of the residents I was acquainted with, largely offset by the convenience of having no maintenance of their residences to worry about. And the simplicity of entertaining, combined with the mutually accepted lessening of social obligations, further reduced the environmental stress on these individuals.

Nature

Nature was one topic which always served me well as an "ice breaker" with Ponds residents. Part of the allure of this place is its integration with its natural surroundings. The facility is situated on the grounds of a former country estate. The architect who designed the residence units (a former student of Frank Lloyd Wright, as already noted) endeavored to blend the buildings in with the bucolic landscape rather than attempting to have them dominate it. A small stream flowing from the marshes on the edge of the perimeter road is dammed to form a small lake (Skunk Pond) which is home to a rich water-based ecology.

During the summer, there were dozens of painted turtles perched on every available projection above the waterline soaking up the sun. An occasional snapping turtle floated on the surface of the lake, which also supports a healthy population of "sunnies" and, it is said, large mouth bass, below the patches of water lilies. There were noisy Frogs among the cattails and water weeds and an ever-changing assortment of birds fishing the lake's large minnow population. And there were always lots of Mallard ducks and Canada geese milling about.

Skunk Pond approximately divides the Ponds property into two parts. The lake is spanned by a wide bridge - with huge windows - which is entirely enclosed and completely climate-controlled. The bridge has hand rails on either side, and its flooring is covered with wall to wall carpeting. It is also provided with a comfortable seating area - furnished with couches and easy chairs - midway across its span.

For Ponds residents, this light drenched little alcove was, possibly, the most popular of the facility's several cozy community lounge areas. There were almost always two or three individuals on the bridge basking in the sun, taking in the natural vistas and watching the daily ritual of Ponds staff feeding stale bread to the ducks and the turtles.

It was Dr. Ray Norton, a retired MD who moved to the Ponds from a wealthy suburb in northern New Jersey, who brought my attention to the possibility of a relationship between stage of life and a fascination with one's natural surroundings. It was his feeling that,

> "...elderly people at some point in their lives, no matter what their profession and how far it removed them from contact with nature, want to somehow return to 'mother earth'."

He and his wife Millie had spent a lot of time, with the consent of Ponds management, virtually duplicating – albeit in a scaled-down version - the view they had had from their large suburban home with its decorative plantings, slate terrace, brick wall etc. Dr. Norton told me that they both spent many hours during the warmer months gardening and relaxing on their patio.

I began then to detect a pattern in my conversations with residents indicating that the abundance of "nature" at the Ponds had been a major factor in their initial decisions to reside here. And once here, many of these same individuals began writing about the natural surroundings (via, for example, messages on community bulletin boards or stories and columns in *The Ponder*, the resident newspaper), conversing with each other about them and "communing" with them in various ways.

One "natural" happening which took place while I was there was the birth - next to Heron Pond, a second body of water on the property - of six black swan cygnets. The community seemed captivated. There were daily briefings posted on the bulletin board next to the entrance to the main dining room, there were "backgrounder" stories about swan life cycles in *The Ponder*, and there were those residents, such as Harvey and Merin Coulter, who took it upon themselves to keep the general population verbally updated on the progress of the infants. When one of the cygnets was attacked by a stray dog, it was driven to a local veterinarian, and, when it later died, a sense of gloom seemed to pervade the community.

The Coulters were big fans of the Ponds outdoors. Harvey Coulter, who had headed up the research division of one of the country's largest media corporations for a good part of his working life, had now replaced his focus on corporate matters with his careful observations of the indigenous Ponds wildlife. He had urged the Ponds administration to place a Bluebird house on the property to encourage a resident population of these birds, even though they had not been sighted locally for several years; Mr. Coulter predicted the imminent return of these birds. He also reported seeing deer on the property during his early morning walks with Merin around the facility's perimeter.

Minerva Beasley, the founder of the community's house organ, *The Ponder*, was in her 21st year of residency at the Ponds when I was there. Although not much more than a one page gossip sheet initially, the paper had evolved under Mrs. Beasley's editorship, into a diverse and interesting publication which carried brief summaries of national news stories - particularly those addressing issues important to the elderly - as well as resident contributions of prose and poetry and all of the local "goings on".

The resident contributions were as often focused on the surrounding flora and fauna as they were on the human activities. And Mrs. Beasley herself, was very much involved both with the care and maintenance of the resident's decorative garden and with the cataloging of the native wild flowers, of which she informed me there were at least 35 varieties on the Ponds grounds.

Jerry Sizor was a quiet, friendly man who always seemed interested in what I was doing and what I had to say. He enjoyed reminiscing too, mainly about his background as an AT&T line supervisor dating back to the days when the first long distance telephone lines were being strung around the nation. But Mr. Sizor's current interests lay in his natural surroundings. He talked about the robins returning each spring and the blue jays and the blue birds and the cardinals and even about the groundhog he had spotted.

Mr. Sizor's real fascination, however, was with the many grand old growth trees which dotted the Ponds landscape. He told me that he tried to walk the grounds every day. He had mapped the location of every large tree on the property, and it seemed to me that he viewed each one as a personal "friend". Mr. Sizor was a walking botanical reference book when it came to these trees. He knew their life cycles, their pests and diseases, their approximate ages and just about anything else a body might want to know about a big old tree.

But much of residents' interest in the outdoors was focused on their own small terraces. Desmond South, was high level publishing executive who at one time or another had sat on 27 different boards of directors. Although now in his late 80's, he still made the two hour commute to one of his three offices in New York City about once every other week (he had made the trip twice a week up until his recent hip replacement). But he admitted that his real joys were cooking and gardening. Like Dr. Norton, he had convinced the Ponds administration to let him modify the landscaping immediately behind his apartment. Mr. South had had the standard Ponds shrubbery surrounding his terrace removed and had replaced it with 16 Ramapo tomato plants ("...the Rutgers tomatoes get the blight." he told me). He used the tomatoes for cooking and as gifts to friends and family.

Dr. William and Nellie Winford had turned their patio area into an elaborate Japanese garden. The garden, which had a 300 year old sculpture of a Japanese god at its center, was fringed with various miniature trees, including a weeping crab apple and a dwarf apricot.

Steve Harris fed the wild birds from a large bird feeder on his terrace. He told me that, because of the bird seed which fell to the ground, he also had an occasional rabbit and lots of squirrels as visitors.

Helen Cousins, who was my 96 year old next door neighbor, spent almost every afternoon, weather permitting, on her back patio. She was in constant communication with the grounds keepers, letting them know when she felt the grass needed mowing and letting them know which were the male and which were the female oak trees. One afternoon I heard Mrs. Cousins complaining to Jennie, her companion, that she had actually seen a raccoon steal the banana she had left on her porch chair that afternoon.

These are just a few of the creative uses of residence "backyards" which I found at the Ponds. Many people here seemed to love to get their hands in the soil whether through decorative gardening, growing vegetables or nursing plants in the facility's greenhouse.

And virtually every resident I spoke with had a fascination with the local animal life. Within the focus and limitations of my research, it is risky for me to jump to any broad conclusions concerning this circumstance. As a participant observer of this community, however, Dr. Norton's "back to mother earth" observation seemed feasible to me.

The Return To Mother Earth

But, inevitably, there was the matter of death. My research at the Ponds was not focused, at least not in any preconceived manner, on death or dying *per se*. I was not naïve enough, however, to think that the topic would not arise in a community of people with and average age of 83 and a significant minority in their late 90's. With this demographic, death was obviously one of the things that this population had to deal with regularly (there were five resident deaths during the relatively short time that I lived there).

In the end I approached my research into the nature of death at the Ponds from a number of perspectives, including: 1. Residents' attitudes concerning their decisions to enroll themselves in this sort of community; one which would, in all likelihood, be their final place of residence, 2. The role of community activism vis-à-vis right to die and related issues, 3. Residents' views concerning their own deaths, and 4. How the Ponds as an institution acknowledges the realities of the deaths and dying of its residents.

I was fortunate in the fact that there was precedent research of this topic in the work of Victor Marshall (1980: 153), a Canadian Sociologist who had developed the notion of an individual's death as the culmination – successful or not - of his or her life's "story". He derived this position at least partially as the result of his interviews with Ponds residents in the mid 1970's. He noted that, at the Ponds,

80

"...the administration left the residents free to develop their own responses to death as a community event (Marshall 1975a, 1975c), and the residents began to do so within a year of the founding of the community. Their existence as a 'community of the dying' was openly recognized in the community-run newspaper, and a procedure for discretely announcing deaths on a bulletin board was initiated. The residents developed a low-key but matter-of-fact way of managing death and dying and provided mutual support for the bereaved, while assuring themselves that their own deaths would be handled with similar compassion, dignity and care."

To be perfectly candid, I was uncomfortable with the topic initially. I knew that first hand data would be extremely helpful to me, as an aspiring anthropologist, in my attempts to understand "who these individuals thought they were" as a community and as a peer group. But, I was also worried that my bringing up the topic of death, whether during planned interviews or during impromptu conversations, might well be taken as an invasion of privacy. As with others of my preconceptions, I was both right and wrong.

The truth is that some residents – a significant minority in fact - seemed anxious to talk about the short term inevitability of their own deaths, while others, mainly those viewing the Ponds as a sort of "new start", were not at all receptive to the notion of the Ponds as their "final residence" (or as Jerry Bradford, head of Ponds maintenance was fond of saying, "the last stop", or, "the place you never leave").

Arlene Wallace, a charter resident, was representative of the former position. She told me that she felt that, "...people come here to face their deaths." Daria Peters was another. She hated being old and found it depressing to live in a place where she knew she was going to die. She said that she knew that death was foremost in people's minds here and she was surprised that it had not come up more during my interviewing.

And Flora Mortenson, a resident who never failed to speak her mind, made no bones about her feelings on the subject; she came right out and said to me, "...the trouble with this type of institution is that people are always dying, including friends."

Conversely, however, some, like Harvey and Merin Coulter, viewed their residence at the Ponds as one of convenience; having no worries about their medical care and insurance allowed them to "get on with their lives", age be damned. And then there were the planners like Mrs. Cousins, who, in her mid 90's, knew that the end wasn't too far away no matter what her attitude was. According to Jennie Reed, her aid and companion, Mrs. C.,

> "...has all of the accessories she wants to be buried in chosen and set aside. She has been bugging me to buy her a custom-tailored black velvet dress specifically for the viewing prior to her cremation and the scattering of her ashes at sea among the racing sailboats."

I found that some of the residents had taken an extremely organized approach to the inevitability of their deaths. Hannah Roamer had an inoperable brain tumor and was expected to die in something under a year. Her husband Henry, was suffering dementia and had been permanently relocated to the nursing care unit. Because their deaths were imminent, they had put all of their affairs in order and planned frequent visits with family and friends. Mrs. Roamer was obviously very disturbed by her dilemma, but she had, in her own words, "grabbed it by the horns" and was dealing with it "straight on" rather than denying it or moping around feeling sorry for herself.

The Gelby's, on the other hand, had been planning their eventual residence in a retirement community ('buying into the concept" as Ed Gelby put it) for the eighteen years prior to their admittance to the Ponds. As with many other Ponds residents, their interest derived from the difficult time they had had caring for their own parents in advanced old age, and their desire not to impose themselves on their children

Since the days of Marshall's study, the situation at the Ponds had changed to some degree, but death, for the most part, had remained a discrete, private matter rather than a community affair. There was still no ritual surrounding residents' deaths (I had learned of the deaths which occurred during my stay through conversations with floor staff, casual mentions in overheard conversations among residents or from the very low key postings on the quad bulletin board). At the request of the House Committee, all commemorative plaques honoring deceased Ponders had been removed from all of the common areas.

There were no funeral services or bereavement gatherings on premises (no chapel had been built at the Ponds because the administration felt that too many funeral services would be bad for morale), and no obituaries in the small house organ; only, as Marshall noted, small announcements of passings on the community bulletin board. Most residents checked the bulletin boards daily for lunch and dinner menus, planned events and activities and the deaths of their peers; there were few outward signs that any one of these information categories was of more interest than any of the others.

A significant number of residents were active, mainly through their elected resident committee representatives, in lobbying the State Governor to sign right to die laws which had already been approved by the state's legislators. Gerry Majors and Allie Rush, for example, were two of the most vocal of the resident "activists". They were concerned with living wills and with making sure everyone at the Ponds, including the medical staff, would be receptive to the wishes of those not wanting to stay alive through unnatural or "heroic" means. The Ponds own Dr. Yount supported living wills, but made it clear that he was against euthanasia; he also wondered if residents' awaremess of people dying around them intensified their fears of their own fate.

I found out during a conversation with her in her apartment that Mrs. Majors, who was 95 and who had been at the Ponds for 20 years, had ulterior motives for her desire to die without undergoing attempts to resuscitate her. She was anxiously awaiting her own death. As she put it,

> "I am sick of my old body. I believe in reincarnation, and I believe that through successive reincarnations I will be continually evolving toward something better, and I will ultimately be and see everything".

Similarly, Ginnie Kennon, a new resident whose husband - the former head of a giant national retail chain - had died 12 years earlier, made no bones about her aversion to staying around to suffer the advanced infirmities of old age. Mrs. Kennon told me,

> "I believe in quality of life, not quantity, and [because of the bad experience she had of nursing her father through advanced dementia in his final years] I want someone to pull the plug when my mind goes."

A related issue at the Ponds was the absence of a hospice care unit for the terminally ill. A number of the residents were vocal about their desire for such a unit, and the daughter of one of the residents who had recently died, petitioned Jim directly on behalf of her deceased mother. Although the administration had no philosophical problems with such a facility, Jim pointed out to me that it would be far too expensive for the Ponds to undertake on its own because it would require a dedicated and specially-trained trained staff 24 hours a day, seven days a week.

Finally, nurses, nurses aids and other "hands on" caregivers at the Ponds had their own unique perspectives concerning the deaths of residents, some of whom they had know and closely bonded with over the years. Although the more experienced floor staff were routinely involved with the medical "mechanics" of death as geriatric professionals, I observed that they were in no way immune to its emotional impact, especially when it involved the death of a resident "friend". For example, Tammy Carson, an RN who divided her time between the nursing care unit and the mobile intermediate care team told me,

> "The death certificate never shows it, but everyone dies differently. It used to bother me, but now I enjoy being their and holding their hand when they go."

And Sarah Langley, who was in charge of resident activities at the nursing care unit said that she made an effort to not get too attached to residents because she knew they would not live very long (she had most recently been in Dr. Yount's office when one of her charges went into cardiac arrest and, shortly thereafter, died). There were numerous variations on the theme, but, in the end, even the floor staff who joked with their peers about the humor sometimes associated with the circumstances surrounding resident deaths, were obviously often affected emotionally by it.

Although death was obviously a part of this community, it did not hang over it like a black cloud. At the Ponds both the subject of death and its actuality were treated seriously, dispassionately, sometimes even humorously, but almost never despairingly.

Resident Profiles

During my residency at the Ponds, I classified and categorized the resident body in numerous ways. I broke the group down by age, by former residency, by former occupation, by length of residency, by sex and by almost every other statistical measure I could think of. But what turned out to be the most interesting for me and the most useful to me as a basis for sub-categorizing this community, was the *de facto* manner in which the residents seemed to group themselves.

This revealed itself through their political points of view, the people they chose to socialize and not socialize with, the degree of their participation in the day to day governance of the community, the types of social activities they took part in, the length of time they had resided there and so on. What I came up with was five general categories: The Original Settlers, The Village Elders, The New Turks, the Real Visitors and The Outliers.

The titles of these categories are not entirely whimsical in that they are indicative of how residents actually <u>used</u> the community and how they affiliated themselves. Many Ponds residents could easily fit into more than one of these groupings, and one grouping, The Outliers, is only defined as such by default, as it includes those residents who didn't fall into any other of the four categories.

Because the designations are not mutually exclusive, there are instances when, for example, an individual labeled as a Village Elder may, in fact, also be an Original Settler. In these cases I have picked the designations which I feel most accurately describe the person's point of view or social affiliation rather than, for example, his or her length of residency. These categories worked well for me as a means for explaining individual's attitudes and behavior. What I hope to provide for the reader in the following four chapters is a brief glimpse into the personalities and life views of some of the individuals I have "placed" into each of the above classifications.

These chapters are focused on a sampling of the Ponds residents who had managed to adjust, in various ways, to this specialized environment. Those I have selected from among the dozens I came to know there seem to me to be among the most typical and therefore representative of the groups to which I have consigned them. The compilations are based on my in-depth interviews and day to day interactions with the people described. These residents had achieved a level of "socialization" to this lifestyle through, at least partially, their associations with others who were like them; like them not in just the socio-economic sense or because of similar professional backgrounds, but like them culturally and politically as well.

These vignettes, where ever possible, are built around the words of the informants themselves to allow the reader a sense of what they were really "like" as people. In the end, the residents are what make the Ponds the kind of place that it is and was, and they constitute the backbone of this study.

Chapter Five

The Original Settlers

As already mentioned, the original mission of the Ponds was to provide a moderately-priced, total care retirement community favoring former educators and civil servants. As the result, many, if not most of the original Ponds residents (a.k.a. the "Original Settlers") fit that description. Although the majority now were women, the percentage of married couples had once been higher than with the more recent admissions because the average age of entry was several years younger in those early days (i.e. late 60's to mid 70's vs. mid 80's).

I learned through my interviewing that the charter residents had more of a sense of "community" deriving from, at least partially, their similar professional backgrounds, and their common interest in education, the arts and the humanities. In this regard, I encountered frequent referrals to the "golden days" and to a "civility" among residents, more formal evening attire, silver and china place settings, after dinner resident piano concerts, afternoon teas etc. This, some looked upon as a reward for their years of altruistic service.

As one resident, **Harriet Lesser** said to me,

> "These were the 'golden years', the years when most of the residents were teachers, librarians etc., people of modest means and those of us who haven't had servants but who have served...I found out that we were 'guinea pigs' in a sense because the facility needed a certain number of people of modest means in order to obtain its original certification. I am now partially subsidized, or I couldn't afford it."

Mrs. Lesser had had a career as a high school teacher. She began as a substitute teacher in Ringwood, NJ while she was still a student herself in the New York school system at New Paltz. During World War II she had volunteered as a plane spotter (she told me that she had seen three American Hellcats make emergency landings during her "tour"). Mrs. Lesser had never married because, she told me,

> "I hate cooking, and my most serious suitor gave me a big frying pan for a present."

She came to the Ponds in her 60's, immediately after her retirement, because of debilitating arthritis.

Mrs. Lesser said that,

> "I am quite happy with Jim and the current Ponds administration. This is the seventh administration since I arrived; the others were far less experienced and they were here during financially more difficult times."

In response to my prompt the told me,

> "I am also happy with the entertainment and stimulation provided by the place, particularly the ballet and choral groups from our village neighbors. And I adore the loving and kind medical care I am receiving at the Ponds. I find it hilarious that the Ponds, in its infancy, had to 'steal' three nursing care residents from Monte Vista, its sister CCRC, in order to attain the necessary physician-patient ratio to keep its nursing unit certification."

Mrs. Lesser's biggest problem with the Ponds it seemed was the lack of empathy she perceived in the residents toward those of their fellow residents with physical ailments, particularly those who required the aid of wheelchairs and walkers, and those from the nursing care unit who were referred to as the "screamers" (this was a highly charged issue at the Ponds).

Concerning the newer residents, Mrs. Lesser said,

> "There is a large percentage of people from Peterstown [the nearby, upscale university town] who form cliques and who feel superior to the rest of the residents. I don't attempt to interact with them because I feel inferior just being a teacher. It is harder to get people to volunteer for things now, they feel they are through with that sort of thing in their lives.
>
> The charter group was here when they were much younger and when everything and everyone was new. They created the structure and the rules. The newer ones don't seem to like the young staff like Katie Bee; they find fault with them. I don't like the older staff because they are too stuck in the groove, while the younger ones bring change and innovation.
>
> I also have a lot of respect for the women residents who were formerly members of The League of Women Voters, because of their in-depth, non-political assessments of teacher candidates in their communities and their dissemination of that information to the community."

This latter observation was of interest to me because, I found that several of the members of the group I refer to as "The New Turks" had been active in this organization. There was a certain commonality of commitment to public service between the Original Settlers and The New Turks, even though the members of the two groups were not, for the most part, from similar socioeconomic backgrounds. All in all, I found Mrs. Lesser to be an earthy, unpretentious lady who

90

didn't consider herself to be anything more than an ex-public servant.

Nellie Steiger, well into her 90's, was the quintessential Original Settler in that she had lived her whole life in Hightown and had been very close to the Talcot family who were the original owners of the Ponds guest house - built in by that family in 1929 - and its surrounding property. She told me that,

> "The Hightown area was largely potato farms until the 1950's. Several large corporations set up headquarters here after the construction of the turnpike, which allowed commutation from the New York City area."

She told me that she had become quite ill three years previous to her residence at the Ponds and had been committed permanently to the nursing care facility; her husband had died five years before her commitment.

> "Now when our friends stay in the guest house, they will talk about staying in Uncle Will and Aida's room instead of Blanche and Katherine's room. I used to swim in the upper end of Skunk Pond. My father owned the property next to the Preskill School golf course but he sold it because he didn't have the resources to maintain it. I came to the Ponds in 1970 when my husband retired and we realized that we didn't want the hassle of maintaining our house anymore. The house was originally built in 1898 by my husband's grandfather."

Mrs. Steiger was a graduate of a small upstate New York liberal arts college; she had taught high school chemistry and physics for a short time after her graduation. During our conversations Mrs. Steiger frequently referred to herself as

91

"less broadened" because she had, "always lived around here." She also told me, however,

> "I think of myself as a sort of pioneer because my sister and I were the first women in my family to go to college, and I was the first woman in my family to drive a car, in 1910 when I was 14. I used to be an avid gardener and a dedicated croquet player, but now, I enjoy just sitting around. I feel myself very fortunate to be at the Ponds. I had no real adjustments to make since my friends, family and home were right here anyway."

And as to her family and friends,

> "I have two children, six grand children and 5 great grand children, all of whom visit me regularly. Although most of my friends are gone, I still have a few who come from the residence units to visit me."

When I mentioned the "golden years" referred to by her fellow Original Settlers, Mrs. Steiger told me she believed that that view (she used the phrase "tea and white gloves") had its origins in the fact that the first residents were younger.

Dr. Ardsley Wayans was a tall, stern looking gentleman with white hair and wire rim glasses. He was not a medical doctor, but rather a PhD in chemistry. He had taught chemistry at New York University, but left that position because of the low pay, and took a job with a large consumer products company. He then returned to school to earn a law degree. This put him in a unique position to move rapidly up the executive ladder with his company, which was a producer of food, chemicals and household products. The FDA was just beginning to require product content and warning labels on consumer products, he informed me, and he understood both the chemical and legal aspects of the business.

Although I was initially somewhat intimidated by Dr. Wayans rather staid public demeanor, I found, on getting to know him, that he was a very nice and a very wise man. Dr. Wayans and his wife came to the Ponds when he was only 67; he was one of the facility's charter residents. They had been living in a six room apartment in Queens before his company relocated to suburban New Jersey, where he had lived in a large house.

At about this time, they purchased an acre and a half of property on a mountain ridge in a semi-rural area of New Jersey where they planned to build their "dream" retirement home. He told me though,

> "We were having a hard time with the tradeoff between the maintenance of a large house and our desire to travel. Also, my mother, who was in her 80's, wanted to enter a retirement community like this one, only on a smaller scale, in South Carolina. She found out though that she had waited too long to meet the entrance medical requirements. This started us thinking about our own situation."

The Wayans read about retirement communities in a *New York Times* article and they decided to "poke around".

> "We found out about the Ponds after a visit to a traditional retirement village on the New Jersey shore and decided to have a look at it. After several trips to the Ponds, we were very interested, but we still hesitated to make the commitment. It was the real silver table service and the old world ambiance which finally persuaded us that the place was right for us, but we still wanted to wait another year to two before making the move.

At this time, however, the Ponds marketing rep informed us that there was only one more of the larger three room apartments we liked left in this first stage of the construction; otherwise we would have to wait another five years until the completion of stage two. We decided to sign up, take a three month around the world cruise - using up a large accumulation of my 'comp' days - and then make the move."

He continued,

"If it had been two years instead of five, we would have waited. I didn't find the transition difficult in terms of either leaving friends or because of the reduced space. We had moved residences enough so that we didn't have a group of really long term friends in any one place, and, because of the apartment living we had already had in New York, the reduced space didn't present a problem either. I was easing into semi-retirement by working one day a week less each year. Then I went over into consulting as an independent agent, both for my old company and for others. After our world cruise though, I decided to retire."

The good doctor, it turned out, had some fascinating views concerning retirement, wisdom and old age. In fact, he was a philosopher of more than just chemistry when it came to the elderly in modern society, and he was a virtual historian when it came to retirement communities. He believed that many elderly "just plain don't want to face the fact that they are getting older". One such person, he felt, was his 59 year old son who was an attorney and who still lived in a big house in Westchester County even though his youngest daughter was already out of college.

"It is the biggest psychological problem, and one which has been the least studied. This is the negative side of aging. It amounts to people deceiving themselves. They no longer see things as they are. And as for old people being a source of accumulated 'wisdom', if they weren't wise in middle age, they won't be wise in old age."

And when I mentioned the esteem given to elders in simpler societies, he said,

"In primitive societies, they generally don't live as long, so that the ones that do are oddities and are valued because they are rare. A truly wise person is a 'rare bird' because wisdom, as with scientific method, involves the notion of building on the past, not 'freezing' some particular period of the past. Some people grow old gracefully and some don't. In any event, at some point the mind has just run the course and gives out like any other muscle."

Dr. Wayans told me that the original concept of the Ponds was to develop a "very nice" residential community first and then attach the services – health care, maintenance etc. – onto it. He also informed me that,

"There are quite a few places like Rosemont [where he had formerly resided], with its golf course, tennis courts etc., which are specifically designed for the pre-Ponds 'young group' (mid 60's to late 70's); this will have the effect of keeping the average age of the Ponds' [i.e. the total care retirement facility] higher. I don't believe that the Marriots and the Hyatts are providing the full, true CCRC option. I believe that they are providing instead a 'cafeteria' of services available at people's discretion rather than bundled as they are at the Ponds where no matter what happens you are taken care of."

Dr. Wayans also predicted that the for-profit corporations would be hard pressed to provide the same quality of services as the non-profit ones. He did believe, however, that hotel management training was essential to running CCRC's well, and he said that he hoped that hotel management training schools such as Syracuse would send people to train at places like the Ponds. And as to the future of the Ponds, he said,

> "I personally don't want the Ponds to evolve into a nursing home with a residence attached. I want ambulatory people coming here for the life style, not for the medical care. I had a hard time giving up the apartment in Queens, and considered saving it for retirement. The adjustment to the Ponds was harder for my wife than for me."

Dr. Wayans seemed to have accepted his age limitations, but he also seemed to be enjoying his life at the Ponds. Although he had once been an avid gardener, he now realized that he had to do much less, and he told me, "I just putter around for about 15 minutes". The same applied to his wife's love of cooking. He also loved to read, however, and was in the process of re-reading some of the classics, which, he informed me, "I get much more out of it now that I am older and more experienced myself." He said,

> "The Ponds has all the advantages of having a house full of servants and having a hospital in your backyard without the aggravation of hiring them, supervising them or bothering with any of the details."

He told be that the most formative years of his life (also the best years) were when he was working as an assistant to a sanitary engineer – one of the first practicing ones ever – in the South, where he lived at the time; the man was a "self-made, well-read man." Dr. Wayans was also very proud of

96

the contribution he had made to the science of labeling through mayonaise (the first product to be consistently and universally labeled), his work with the FDA etc. But, surprisingly, he was neither active in his former profession, nor much interested in it in its current state of development.

He did reminisce about his former travels though, particularly his 1985 trip to Russia - where he rode in a boat for eight days toward the Black Sea - at the time when Gorbachov was just coming into prominence. He didn't seem to miss the travel very much though; the reminiscence seemed to be enough.

Minerva Beasley came to the Ponds in 1968 – one year after its founding - at the age of 68. Although born and raised in Brooklyn, she had spent most of her active career years as an English and speech teacher in Basking Ridge, New Jersey. After coming to the Ponds, Mrs. Beasley began working for the then editor of *The Ponder* .

> "Then I took over *The Ponder* as editor after a year or two and changed it from a 'gossip sheet' to a diverse paper with real community news, original poetry and prose etc. I invented a humorous character I called 'Newberry Miner' from a mistaken pronunciation of a resident name. I also added the column of an amateur philosopher named Ralph Alexander. I love to write poetry or, as I call them, 'ditties', which come to me while I am walking around the premises."

Mrs. Beasley and her good friend Sally Bergen loved discussing the "old days" at the Ponds, and contrasting the charter residents to the newer ones:

> "There was a different type of resident in the first batch; more professionals, more community spirit. The new group has more money, more 'country

club types'; still professionals, but not as many, and it is less academic. And now the administration allows more of the infirm in, which isn't fair for the current residents because the costs go up for everybody. The new group, because they are older and less well, are not energetic enough to take over tasks from others as they age. And the new bunch has less community spirit."

Like many of the other residents in the Original Settler group, Mrs. Beasley had happy memories of the early days of the community:

> "There were card games, sing- alongs, New Years Eve parties, "elegant" coffee hours with beautiful china demitasse cups, piano playing in the dayrooms, and the 35 different kinds of wild flowers growing on the Ponds property. I remember the introduction of six wicket croquet, and the thrill of the visit by Archbishop Fulton Sheen."

Dr. Phillip Merton was an 85 year old Protestant minister who had lived at the Ponds for 19 years,18 of those as the facility's resident clergyman. He had earned his Ph.D. degree in philosophy and religion from an Ivy League university with the intention of teaching, but had found that his real interests and talents lay in preaching. When we first met, he walked me through the history of his theological commitment:

"Although I was brought up as a Presbyterian, I was ordained in the First Congregationalist Church. I changed denominations in order to obtain my own ministry, because I would have been a 'third fiddle' in the much larger Presbyterian Church.

After my ordination, I was a minister in Hasbrook Heights, New Jersey for 12 years, then Albion,

Connecticut for three years. I left the latter position because the Catholics ran the schools and I didn't want my children exposed to their instruction. I relocated to Van Nuys, California, re-joined the Presbyterian Church and practiced there until my retirement at the age of 65.

After only two weeks at another retirement village in Southern New Jersey, I was asked by the Ponds to be its resident preacher, in return for a reduction in my monthly fees."

Dr. Merton was a prolific painter. He had taken lessons with several well known artists, and his paintings were frequently on exhibit and for sale at the Ponds. Because he was not a wealthy man, the proceeds from the sale of his paintings helped him meet his living expenses. He told me that he had traveled extensively throughout Europe, Mexico and the United States. Since leaving the ministry, he claimed to have become quite "overtly liberal" . He said,

"I am actively involved in local groups promoting nuclear non-proliferation and world peace. I think I have to attribute my recently found liberalism to the 'new energy' I have derived from being free of my obligations to the conservative Presbyterian church."

When I brought up the notion of the Ponds' "golden years" to Dr. Merton, he concurred with that designation. Of those early years, he said,

"Those were 'golden years' in the sense that there was a much stronger feeling of community spirit. Church attendance is down with the newer group because they are wealthier - more Episcopalians - and more concerned with their privacy. They don't want anything critical or controversial published in

The Ponder [the resident – published newspaper], which I found out when I wanted to submit something to it. I preach sometimes now at Monte Vista [another member of the Christian Homes group], and I find that the people there feel that Ponds residents are snotty and feel superior, and I have to agree with them."

He liked Jim and the current administration, but he felt that the absence of a third physician was a problem.

"And the problem is exacerbated because the female physician who was sent by the Ponds to Monte Vista was so overloaded that she had to send residents back to the Ponds for medical attention. I was personally affected by the vacancy in that my annual March physical seemed to be indefinitely delayed."

As I was leaving his apartment, Dr. Merton told me, apparently apropos of nothing other than the joy he took in it,

"I am the honorary grandfather of two girls who are the daughters of the marriage of a Dutch man and a Lebanese woman. The mother died and the children are taking it badly, so I have to spend time to help them. I am going to Nova Scotia for a trip with my son in August."

Most of these original residents also admitted to some problems in the early years too, however. When the fees at the Ponds began going up to cover the unforeseen costs of increased resident longevity, the then head of the Resident Forum Committee, Peter Overton, attempted to force the facility into receivership. The case went away - because it was apparently based purely on supposition as to the need for and use of resident fees – but it came to represent for

100

many, a significant turning point in the future course of the community.

It was at about this juncture that certain of the more willful residents, those accustomed to managing others and to "running their own shows", so to speak, began asserting their authority through the increased number and influence of resident committees. This group, consisting of both original residents and newer arrivals, is the one that I have chosen to refer to as The Village Elders.

Chapter Six

The Village Elders

A significant minority of individuals who I have designated collectively as the Village Elders (the Elders), were, like the Original Settlers, among the first Ponds residents. Although the charter residents within this group almost invariably reminisced about the "golden days", they were generally much more proactive than the Original Settlers in terms of their participation in the governance of the place. Some had been involved with the creation of the original resident committees, and they (or their elected stand-ins) still either headed or were active in the more substantive of these committees.

I identified other residents as Village Elders even though they were not residents of the original resident body. These individuals had often been mentored by their more tenured peers within the group, and had come to accept most of the group's positions on matters concerning the facility's protocols.

Other residents came to the Elders for advice concerning their rights as 'tenents', or concerning problems they were having with the Ponds administration. Conversely, Jim and his staff used the Village Elder group as a sounding board for proposed management policy changes, with the assumption that if the changes were acceptable to the Elders, they could be "sold" to the rest of the resident body.

The Elders were generally politically and socially conservative and highly protective of their "turf". Many seemed to feel that the Ponds was already "as good as it gets", and they expected to be consulted about all community matters of any consequence, particularly those which threatened change to any of their long standing "traditions".

Because **Dr. Effie Brontman** was the quintessential Village Elder, I have dedicated a little bigger piece of the pie here than I have to some of her less 'stereotypical' peers. With a Ph.D. in Library Science, she had worked for many years at a premier university in the Northeast as head librarian for the institution's prestigious college of medicine.

Dr. Brontman was a published, highly respected academic (in fact, I was told by another resident, that she was one of the top 10 medical librarians in the United States) who believed in the virtual infallibility of the scientific method, and who applied that method to most of what she was involved with at the Ponds. I was informed by another long term resident that, "you just plain don't make changes in the protocol of the place without first consulting with Dr. Brontman."

Her most significant contribution to the community had been a series of taped, in-depth interviews which she had conducted with Ponds residents more than a decade prior to my being there. A primary objective of these interviews had been to poll resident feelings about the Peter Overton "scandal" mentioned in the previous chapter (i.e. the attempt by the then chairman of the Resident Forum Committee, Mr. Overton, to force the Ponds into receivership over the facility's rapidly increasing fees).

But these interviews ended up covering a broad range of topics and offering to the reader a fairly comprehensive look into the "culture" of the community at that stage of its evolution.

The transcribed collection of tapes, which was filed in the resident library for general consumption, was a boon to me in my efforts to understand where the 'movers and shakers' were coming from. I made it a point to review these transcripts prior to each of my own scheduled interviews with members of the residents recorded on the tapes.

I managed to arrange an interview with Dr. Brontman approximately two weeks after I had arrived at the Ponds. During the day prior to our meeting, I spent several hours in the Ponds library reviewing the transcriptions of Dr. Brontman's resident interviews. I was anticipating a rigorous critique of my study objectives and the methodology I planned to use for my research, so I wanted to be very "buttoned up"; very academic.

I decided to give a general direction to the interview by posing three broad areas of discussion: 1. The changes she had observed in the Ponds over the years (e.g. types and attitudes of residents), 2. Her 'take' of the adjustment processes necessary for the successful transition to the CCRC lifestyle, and 3. The notion of statuses within the resident body.

She seemed to like the way I had proposed to enter into our dialogue. When I mentioned my apprehensions about returning to graduate school at the age of 50, she told me that she could empathize because she had taken computer courses with a group one third her age, "…who treated me as if I would break." Just when I was beginning to relax a little, however, she also informed me that,

> "The community didn't 'agree' to have you here, they only deferred to Mr. Daniels, who is better than past directors. There are a number of people who don't want you here, and the only reason that it is acceptable is that participation is strictly voluntary."

With that, she opted to begin our semi-formal interview with my discussion area number one.

Dr. Brontman had some strong opinions about the attitudes of the newer residents at the Ponds. She had recently given a cocktail party for a group of new residents, something she said had become, for the earlier residents, a sort of tradition. These

104

affairs were intended to 'familiarize' new resident with the community and with their new neighbors. She told me that,

> "Most of the attendees were more interested in talking to each other about their mutual acquaintances, clubs, social activities and so on in their former communities than about the Ponds and their new neighbors. Newer residents don't want to get involved with forum committees or even with many of the group activities of the community. I think that part of this is because of the increased age and physical condition of the new residents which, in turn, relates to the Ponds economic concerns."

I mentioned to Dr. Brontman that one or two of the newer residents I had interviewed complained of a lack of cultural stimulation at the Ponds. She gave me no quarter on this matter:

> "Every kind of intellectual stimulation you could get is here if you reach out for it. I have a library card [at the prestigious university], and I have no trouble interacting with the academic community. We also have our own monthly lecture series here given by residents in their respective fields of expertise. We have covered topics as diverse as whales, NASA, the relationship of art and medicine (mine), Russia and various periods of literature; Jeanne Sandler gave two lectures on that topic."

When I queried the good doctor as to how she found the transition from "civilian" life to the CCRC, she told me that she had come here, as the then youngest resident, with a "...specific, elaborate plan, with various projects." I asked her if she felt that, the CCRC being the final place of residence for most of those coming in, it was a good thing for one to "have a plan". She said,

"This is generally true if the plans are realistic. Also it helps coming in with a group of friends, which seems to be the case with the new residents. The adjustment was somewhat easier for me because I had lived a life of moving around from place to place. Part of the trauma for women formerly active in their communities is the cutoff from transportation for getting back and forth to clubs and organizations and to friends in the community."

Then she referred me to a study of coping written by a Princeton philosophy student. A copy of the study was on file with Jim, she told me, and she would ask that it be made available to me and to interested residents. And when I probed her as to the future of retirement communities such as the Ponds, she mentioned the problem of greatly increased medical costs which was being exacerbated by the increased longevity of CCRC residents.

"If the elderly eat properly and take good care of themselves, they can live practically forever in the Ponds type of environment. I suggest you look at studies from the 1940's and 1950's about the life spans of nuns and monks living cloistered lives, available at the Medical School Library at Columbia.

This increased longevity will cause severe economic squeezes on communities like the Ponds, and will change the character of them in terms of residents vs. patients. You should study different elderly living environments but not seek direct comparison because base variables such as socio-economic status vary so widely."

With this academic counsel, I left our interview feeling that I had passed muster with the most senior of the Village Elders.

My next "target" within the group I had designated as the Village Elders was **Martha Harvey**. When I phoned her, we set up an interview for 2:00 p.m. the following day at her apartment. When I arrived, at precisely 2:00 p.m., her front door was already open; she was sitting on one of the couches in her living room waiting for me. Mrs. Harvey is a very elegant woman, almost imperial in her demeanor, and still quite pretty.

The apartment reflected its owner's refined, upper Park Avenue tastes. Although she was born a Canadian citizen in Toronto in 1911, she spent most of her life in Philadelphia and New York City. She hails from a very prominent publishing family, and both she and her husband – now a full time resident of the nursing facility, but formerly the CEO of a well known firm in that business - have also written and published a number of books on their own.

Mrs. Harvey, as with many of the other charter residents I interviewed, had fond memories of the facility's "golden days", and a few complaints about the more recent arrivals. She attributed the alleged festive environment and camaraderie among the residents of those early day to,

> "…their relatively young age. The average age was in the low to mid 70's in those days. I was the youngest at 59; my husband was 65. We came when my husband retired. He stayed actively involved with his former company in New York, however, and, additionally, worked with recordings for the blind. Before coming to the Ponds we weighed other options.
>
> We considered keeping our estate in Long Island, but decided that with maintenance, snow removal and so on, it wasn't worth it. In those days there was party after party – to the point where you were socially booked three weeks in advance. No one would think

of even asking you without giving at least two weeks notice."

Mrs. Harvey, as with other members of this "group", seemed to resent what she perceived as an increase in the community's medical problems, which she attributed to the advanced age of new Ponds residents (she particularly disliked the growing number of wheel chairs). She also felt that the new arrivals were much less involved with the affairs of the community. By comparison, Mrs. Harvey had always been very much involved with the community, and she was regularly consulted regarding resident policy matters.

She originally participated on various of the forum committees (she still acted as a sort of professor *emeritus* to those committees), and she was currently in charge of all of the crafts and library displays in the hallways off of the quad. Mrs. Harvey was also pioneering the concept of video picnics, which consisted of the breaking of the longer movies shown in the main meeting room into two parts, one before and one after a picnic lunch. She did tell me, however, that,

> "Although I miss the ambience of the 'golden days', I also love the fact that my life is so comfortable, and I don't have to worry about entertaining and going to lots of parties. I love the fact that cocktail parties are kept to one hour and that people head home after dinner. I don't miss my life in New York at all because it is such a strain to entertain, to go to parties, to get cabs, to get competent help and nursing care.
>
> I feel that the air conditioned corridors here are a great aid to the socialization process in terms of being able to move from residence to residence without having to deal with the inclement weather."

Mrs. Harvey came to the Ponds on the advice of a friend who had visited it and raved about it. Her friend had seen it advertised in *The New York Times*.

> "We traveled a lot at first and even used our home in Long Island. We soon realized, however, that everything we were looking for was right here. The spacial transition wasn't too hard because we were used to the confined space of our New York apartment. Almost everyone, including those who move from large estates, adjust very easily, however.
>
> I am very much into croquet; I have been aggressively playing it for 50 years. The residents aren't really fanatical about the competition because they have their own little social croquet groups [which I observed as being extremely competitive] and prefer those to the stress of competition and interaction with people they don't know as well.
>
> I have a group of very good friends, and I feel the influence of [renowned nearby university] on the group on community spirit has been a very positive one in terms of providing a sense of camaraderie and keeping the social life alive. I view the community as a combination of a cruise ship and a girl's camp."

Mrs. Harvey told me that she "loved" the Ponds staff, and that she wished that she could share the benefits of her fortunate economic status ("share my luck" was the way that she put it) with them, even though she understood Jim's policy prohibiting this. All in all, I found Mrs. Harvey to be a thoroughly charming and ingratiating lady.

Carl Saunders, who was the head of the Resident Forum Committee (the mother ship of the whole committee fleet, and by far the most prestigious) while I was at the Ponds, was well liked and respected by most of the resident body. He was a large, gangly man with a sort of "down home" demeanor which encouraged people – me included – to want to befriend him. He was also all business when it came to the affairs of his office, however.

Mr. Saunders was well informed regarding the problems of the elderly, and he felt an obligation to serve not only his fellow Ponds residents, but also his age peers at large. As for the latter, he spent a significant amount of his time in both Washington and in Trenton lobbying for the interests of seniors.

I was introduced to Mr. Saunders by another resident (Flora Mortenson, the widow of a prominent professor of sociology at one of the Ivies) who had taken it upon herself to indentify for me and introduce me to the "decision makers" in the community. Mr. Saunders and I seemed to 'click' right away, and he invited me to visit his apartment/home for a talk the following afternoon.

The Saunders' residence was one of a number of top of the line, highly sought after units at the Ponds. Although it is attached by an extension to the main, glassed-in corridors, it has the feel of a small, stand alone suburban ranch house. Mrs. Saunders, whose nickname is "Binkie", exuded the same easy graciousness as her husband Carl, and was equally passionate regarding the plights of the Ponds community and her fellow seniors at large; she immediately made me feel welcome in their home.

When I commented on how I liked their cottage, Mrs. Saunders told me,

> "We were on the waiting list for nine years before this house became available two years ago. It was one of only two units we were willing to accept before moving to the Ponds. We moved from a home which was smaller than our original home. It was

like this cottage only with an upstairs, so the transition in terms of space was not a hard one [although she did use the term "cramped" and the phrase "right on top of each other" more than once when discussing their adjustment to their new living quarters].

Fifty percent of the people who come here are here because they want to be independent of their children, who are too busy and not equipped to handle the needs of their aging parents."

Related to this, Mr. Saunders also informed me that,

"Sixty percent of the people who come here come on the recommendation of others. Because of this, it is extremely important, whether they know it or not, to keep the residents happy."

Both Mr. and Mrs. Saunders were interested in and well informed about emerging trends affecting the elderly. They freely quoted the statistics they had researched regarding these trends, but they also cited the personal experiences of their friends and fellow residents. He was obviously worried about some of what he was finding out and conveyed to me:

"I am quite concerned about the direction of health care, both in terms of the extent of services being provided, and in terms of the increasing expense, both at the Ponds and in U.S. society at large. I know of someone who can only afford to stay here ten more years. I am also concerned about the residents' understanding of the very complicated contracts they have signed, and I don't feel many of them know exactly what they have committed to or what they are entitled to receive."

Mrs. Saunders too had some problems in this regard. She told me that the peace of mind that she was supposed to receive

from her health insurance wasn't there because she was
unsure of the solvency of the whole place, given the trends in
health care costs. Mr. Saunders, in turn, worried about the
long term solvency of the Ponds by reason of the people in
charge:

> "I am unhappy about the two levels of management
> and about the incompetence at the corporate level. I
> am worried that if the residents become dissatisfied
> they will begin legal proceedings which will result in
> the same factionalization experienced during the
> Overton incident. It is a sort of dilemma in the sense
> that costs will have to go up to cover increased
> medical costs, yet residents will tolerate only a
> certain level of expense increases. Both Binkie and I
> are concerned about the loss of the third doctor, and
> upset by the way it was done."

At this point, Mr. Saunders pulled out the revised plans for the
alternative to "Building 50" (the original proposal for the
intermediate care facility). The plan would move and simplify
the administrative offices, while adding 19 "regulated" units
(nursing care units, whether intermediate or long term, are
staffed by nurses and have to be regulated by the state).

Ten of the new regulated units would be built from existing
independent living units, so the 'net' increase in regulated
units would be less that 10%, and would thus not require re-
certification by the state (a somewhat convoluted way of
avoiding dealing with the state it seemed to me, but, 'heh',
whatever works).

He told me that the plan had been accepted by both the
residents (via the residents' Forum and Intermediate Health
Care Committees) and by the administration, and that ground
would be broken within a year. Mr. Saunders believes that all
CCRC's will offer dedicated intermediate care facilities in the

near future and that the Ponds couldn't possibly remain competitive without one.

The balance of our conversation that afternoon focused generally on the processes of adjusting mentally and physically to the CCRC lifestyle. In this regard, Mrs. Saunders told me that,

> "Coming to the realization that this is the last stage is the hardest thing. And in terms of adjustment, it takes about a year to break old ties, give up the family doctor, the old stores, the restaurants, the service providers and so on. I don't buy the notion that 'having' to do less and 'having to downsize' provides its own rewards. I feel that some of the things I am not doing any more are things which would still add enjoyment to my life."

Conversely, Mr. Saunders, after rattling off a whole list of available Ponds activities, told me that he has more to do at the Ponds than he has time for (she said that that was because he moved so much slower). He also felt that if a died in the wool academic like Dr. Brontman was not lacking in mental stimulation, nobody should be.

About two weeks after this interview I was again invited to the Saunders' home, this time for a small cocktail party. And once again the conversation was largely about the welfare of the elderly and about the viability of the retirement community in light of current medical and economic trends.

The Saunders were seriously nice, serious people who had no intention of dropping out of the mainstream. I learned a lot from them, and I greatly appreciate their contribution to my understanding of some of the important issues affecting their cohort group.

One morning when I was in the main residents' lounge sifting through the large book of resident biographies, an elegantly dressed woman suddenly appeared at the door. She walked briskly across the room, stood directly in front of me and said, with a deep southern drawl, "I am **Melanie Kirk**, and I want to be on the list of interviewees of yours." I knew of her through other residents, and I immediately agreed. When I asked her when it would be convenient for her, her answer was, "What about right now?." It wasn't really a question.

Mrs. Kirk was a renowned figure in the world of social entertaining. She had taught courses in gourmet cooking and gracious entertaining and had published several books on the same subjects. She had been born into a wealthy Missouri family where she lived in great comfort until her marriage to a prominent corporate executive. The marriage ended in divorce 33 years later, leaving Mrs. Kirk – who was 61, and without a college degree or any "work" experience – to fend for herself. She told me,

> "I divide my life into four phases: 1. My premarriage years, living a very upper crust social life, 2. My married life, 3. My life after my divorce, struggling to regain my financial independence through my own efforts, and 4. My post-retirement life here at the Ponds."

She then proceeded to tell me the story of her late life career success.

> "My divorce left me in dire financial circumstances. My only skills were that I played a knockout game of bridge and gave wonderful dinner parties. Although my husband and I had already decided to divorce, we didn't give up our plans for a 150 person dinner party at our home in Fairfield County.

114

At lunch with a friend of mine some time after the party, she asked me who I had hired to arrange the party, because she would like to hire that same caterer. At this point I realized that I might have a marketable talent. I was determined to stand on my own two feet no matter what."

Mrs. Kirk was obviously proud of her reputation and her accomplishments. I was taken by her enthusiasm and I encouraged her to give more of the details to me. She continued,

"I began to take instruction from James Beard and to travel to resorts and restaurants to look at the kitchens and so on. I feel that fate stepped in at some point [her faith in the Methodist Church was very strong I learned]. When I attempted to resign as head of my garden club because of financial considerations, they not only refused my resignation, they insisted I go to Honolulu to represent them at their annual meeting. It turned out that the Japanese government paid for my trip.

It took me two and a half years to gain my confidence and begin to establish my reputation. I started by sending 100 letters to acquaintances – but not to close friends – from which I got 8 responses. During the course of the last 27 years I've had 9,000 students and published three books."

Mrs. Kirk was 88 at the time of that conversation. She had come to the Ponds six years earlier, after everyone in her family – except her two children and six grand children – had died. She had come across the Ponds while looking at the possibility of building a CCRC in Fairfiled County with a group of investors. And, reflecting her natural business acumen, she said,

"I fault them [the Ponds] for taking the very old and the feeble, but I admit that there is a fine line between financial ruin and lower admission standards."

I have included Mrs. Kirk among the Village Elders, in spite of her short tenure at the Ponds, because she was always on the administration's "must see" list when it came to any changes in the Ponds social life. She acted as liaison between the residents and Sal Trematossi, the facility's head chef, and it was said that he never made a significant move without her consultation. But her advice was also sought by other staff members and by residents about all matters involving entertaining.

Mrs. Kirk was a true southern gentlewoman. But although her manners were refined from her upbringing and from years of social interaction with the privileged elite, her demeanor was not one of aloofness. She was friendly and funny and genuinely fun to be with.

Of all the residents I got to know in the Village Elder group, **Helene Koster** was the most outspoken and the most opinionated. She had developed her own system for categorizing residents, most of which was based upon her personal feelings about their "idosyccracies", their professional accomplishment (or lack of it), their ethnic backgrounds, their gender and their conformance to (or not) her own rigid mores and world view.

Mrs. Koster considered herself an intellectual, and, if well read is considered the sole determinant of that designation, she was probably right. She was, after all, a Doctor of Library Science and had been head librarian for many years of what is considered by many to be the most comprehensive library system in the U.S.

Mrs. Koster sort of latched right on to me from the time we first met at my introduction during a Resident Forum

Committee meeting shortly after my arrival at the Ponds. She had approached me about arranging an interview, and she always made it a point to stop me in the hallways to offer advice as to whom I should be interviewing, and as to what "types" of residents lived at the Ponds. Here is a sample of some of her thoughts:

> "Women who have not worked in 9 to 5 jobs as careers [at least two thirds of the Ponds female residents at that time] are not as intellectually involved. Married women [she had never been married] suffer somewhat the same handicap, although unmarried women, like guys, are somewhat out of step with society. There are only about 15 women who have never been married at the Ponds."

When I commented on some of the extraordinary backgrounds of Ponds residents, Mrs. Koster told me,

> "You shouldn't confuse accomplishment with intelligence. In fact, there are quite a number of Ponds residents who are basically stupid ["dumb", "dull", and "uninvolved" are other such adjectives were sprinkled quite liberally throughout her descriptions of her fellow residents]. Bear this in mind, the Ponds is not all intelligent people. There is an enormous range of intellectual aspirations and abilities. I will give you some names in the very strictest of confidence."

She gave me three names at that point and an expanded list at a later date. I was actually asked to burn the list after I had memorized the names. By way of an example of "dumbness", Mrs. K. informed me of the way residents had reacted with total disorientation to administration changes to table seating arrangements in the main dining room. And with regard to male Ponds residents:

"Men adjust [to the CCRC lifestyle] with much more difficulty than women, and some just sit around and do nothing. Mrs. Harvey's husband, unlike Martha [Harvey], who is always thinking of new things to do, began to deteriorate immediately after entering the Ponds. And some men are totally at a loss as to how to act if you invite them over for a drink [here she was referring to unattached males]. They do a fine job at a turkey dinner where the decisions involve white meat or dark. These men are just barely middle class, where the father drinks up most of his paycheck at the pub on paydays."

And as to African Americans and "foreigners",

"All Blacks have a common cultural or ethnic origin. Without Blacks and foreigners the country would have a completely different welfare status. I would have to exclude some of the better accomplished though. For example, who would have thought that a German Jew [she was referring to Carl Saunders] would be the chairman of the Resident Forum Committee? Carl is a unique individual who has risen above his origins to be successful."

But on the subject of the Ponds as an example of the CCRC type community, and concerning Jim's administration, she was mostly approving.

"The Ponds is both a thorn in the side of its parent and a jewel in it's crown because the people here are demanding and discriminating. And the maintenance is expensive. The prior administration just let the maintenance go to hell and didn't have any concerns for the concerns of the residents. We are fortunate, because even though we are living in the day of the proliferating aged, we are also living in the day of the machinery to take care of them.

Other CCRC communities have profited by the mistakes of the Ponds, but not by the benefits of it. I believe that residents must serve the community in order to create a positive image of it, though, and the incoming people aren't doing that. Functions such as my library work will have to be done by professionals in the future."

She was not fond of the incoming residents – who she referred to as the "new money people" and those from the "commercial world" – because they were, in her mind, merely users of the facilities and not contributors to the community.

Conversely, Mrs. Koster was actively involved in expanding and updating the library's card catalogue system. She had divided its collection into "mystery", "other fiction" and "non-fiction"; non-fiction, in turn was divided into "biographies" and "other". She was also involved with groups doing play readings, groups creating various kinds of exhibits and groups producing posters (65 during the previous year she told me).

Although, I was told, she now read considerably slower due to her failing eyesight, and she no longer traveled, she commented,

"I am not overly concerned by this because I've done an enormous amount of reading throughout my life and, like travel, nobody can take your reading experiences away from you. Travel is too difficult now, and the places have most likely changed beyond recognition anyway."

Mrs. Koster invited me to her place for cocktails about two weeks after this interview. Her eclectically-furnished apartment had an almost 1960's Greenwich Village bohemian feel; it looked comfortable and well used. A large work/eating table, almost too big for the dining alcove it was in, had papers and supplies all over it.

There were two massive bonze horses on a side table next to the dining alcove. She told me that she had purchased these in Venice in 1923 and that they had originally been used on the bows of gondolas. A very old pottery chard hung on the wall over her couch next to a pair of sepia-toned photographs of her grand parents. Her balcony was overflowing with plants.

My conversations with Mrs. Koster continued throughout my stay at the Ponds. On a personal level, I had some problems with her overt bigotry toward those she felt to be "different" from her, but I didn't express my opinions on that subject to her. In terms of expedience, she was a good informant. Her insights into the politics and practical workings of the place were very helpful.

She opened up to me, I think, both because my pursuit was an academic one which piqued her intellectual curiosity and because I seemed to have passed her "worthiness" test. I'm not sure how well Mrs. Koster was liked by her fellow residents, but she was definitely a force in the governance of the community. Knowing her was an "experience".

Chapter Seven

The Young Turks

When compared with the Village Elders, the Young Turks were often somewhat younger and most had not resided at the Ponds for as long. Like the Village Elders, many of the Young Turks were impressively credentialed academically. They were also, however, from generally more prominent social backgrounds and were more politically liberal.

This group had a higher percentage of women, especially women who were involved with advocating innovation and change for the community; they were largely interested in the future of the place rather than either maintenance of the status quo or a return to the "golden" days.

These women seemed generally dissatisfied with the level of intellectual stimulation available to them at the Ponds, and with the residents' seeming lack of interest in it as a community. Their push for change often brought them into conflict with both the Village Elders and with Ponds management. Many of them were used to having power within their respective suburban communities (or societal domains) and, more generally, through their own former careers and or through their husbands' prominence. Due to the efforts of the Young Turks, the whole process of the socialization of new residents was changing.

Jeanne Sandler - an attractive, vivacious lady in her late 70's from a prominent New England family - had been at the Ponds only 18 months when I arrived. I first encountered her, just a few days after my arrival, while she was working in the resident library. She apparently recognized me as the "student in residence" and began to talk with me as if we had known each other for years. Mrs. Sandler was in the process

121

of organizing the books by categories and she asked me for my help in reaching one of the higher shelves.

She seemed to take me into her confidence immediately, I believe because I was a fellow academic in her eyes. As for her own scholarly credentials, after receiving her Ph.D. in American Literature at one of the premier Ivy League universities in the late 1940's, (an impressive feat in itself in that day and age), she earned her tenure at another of the 'Ivies', where she became a widely acclaimed Brownian scholar.

In her Ponds library job as Area Chairman in charge of the books in the outlying resident day rooms, Mrs. Sandler worked directly under the supervision of Helene Koster. This became a source of irritation for Mrs. Sandler, and a sort of case study (for me) in the frictions between the Village Elders - in the persons of Mrs. Koster and Dr. Brontman, Mrs. Koster's mentor - and the New Turks.

Mrs. Sandler was in strong, philosophical disagreement with the Brontman-Koster coalition. She felt that,

> "Dr. Broadman [who was in charge of the library's archives] is too taken up with the past as one can see by her continued focus in her taped series of resident interviews. In my opinion, the library and the archives should be consolidated under one chairman, and I also feel that the ultimate responsibility for the filing of both archival materials and the other visual media should be the sole responsibility of the head of the Library Committee.

> With the current system, Dr. Brontman is in charge of the Archives Committee and Mrs. Koster is in charge of the Library Committee. And I am particularly disturbed by the manner in which the archival materials are scattered all over the desk and table

tops; they should be filed on the shelves like everything else."

But I was quickly made aware of her **main** worry with regard to life at the Ponds:

"My biggest concern is the lack of mental stimulation. All of the resources are here in terms of residents' backgrounds, but many are 'over the hill' and no longer mentally or physically alert enough to participate in stimulating discourse."

She had chosen the Ponds over a Quaker run CCRC she had looked at mainly because,

"What I don't like about the Quaker facility is the constant loving care, the insistence on a companion, etc. It seems that they want you to give up your independence or your unique personality."

A week later, Mrs. Sandler called me to invite me to join her for dinner – her treat - in the resident dining room. During the previous week, Mrs. Koster had retired as Chairman of the Library Committee due to a disagreement (with the Ponds administration, I think, but it was never made clear to me) as to the use of the library's resident endowment fund for new acquisitions.

Mrs. Sandler had assumed the chairmanship unchallenged. When I congratulated her on her new position, she told be that she was still upset that she would not have control over the archives.

We talked about leaders and followers and about those with vision concerning the future of the community, and about those who were involved and those who weren't. She told me,

"Some people are doers and some people are followers or talkers. I consider myself to be the former. I have a certain facility for management in that, unlike some who can't balance their checkbooks, I handle all of my own investments and the other details of my life."

And even when admitting to the inescapability of the aging process, she managed to come across as in control:

"I have been mentally planning for the inevitability of my own physical slowdown and infirmity with advancing age. I can't understand how some people in their 80's and 90's presumably are 'surprised' with their own failing resources or with the deaths of their aged acquaintances. Like Mr. Barron's death [a recently deceased Ponds resident] at 93, which seemed to take many by surprise. "

And as to the relationship between age and the downsizing of life,

"Older people make their worlds smaller and smaller until they are left with just their egos and begin taking a possessive attitude toward such things as the community's doctor."

Mrs. Sandler seemed to prove her point on these matters vis-a-vis the almost total lack of success she experienced with her "Ponds Ponders" lectures series. As an example, I refer again to the one lecture in this two or three lecture series that I personally attended, during which I observed that a number of residents had fallen asleep. And there were no questions at all addressed to Mrs. Sandler during the discussion session after the talk. She later admitted to me that she was having a hard time right from the start interesting any of the more prominent residents to discuss their careers in front of an audience.

This turned out to be the final one of these lectures. It seemed to me that many of the residents were no longer interested in the acquisition of more knowledge or with imparting their own knowledge to others in the group. Most wanted to enjoy their new lives at the Ponds and to reminisce quietly, in small groups of close friends, about the long, productive lives they had already lived. That is not to say that Mrs. Sandler's enthusiasm for cultural stimulation was an anomaly. In fact, her concern was a common one among the New Turks.

Flow Harrison was the first resident to approach me after my talk to the Resident Forum Committee. She expressed a real interest in my "project" and asked to be both an interviewee and a consultant. She had been at the Ponds for less than a year at that point. Her husband, a renowned New York orthopedic surgeon, had died several years before Mrs. Harrison came to the Ponds, after suffering a long, debilitating illness, during which Mrs. Harrison had been his primary care giver.

Although she had lived a life of comparative ease in Westchester County, she had also been thoroughly immersed, on a volunteer basis, in an extensive range of social services (Mrs. Harrison had earned her Masters Degree in social service from an excellent New York university). And as a charter member of the League of Women Voters in her district, she tended to have a liberal political bent, which put her at odds from time to time with the generally more conservative resident body at the Ponds.

I set up an afternoon interview with Mrs. Harrison during the third week of my stay at the Ponds. We first discussed when and why she had chosen the Ponds and what she did and didn't like about it:

> "An old friend, Ellie Barnes, who has been a resident for several years, first told me about the

Ponds. I carefully researched the place when I was 70 and finally decided to come here when I was 80. I came here to take care of myself after taking care of a sick mother, a sick husband and a sister with cancer for 11 years.

I have three children with whom I talked about coming here for ten years, but they almost balked at the last moment. They visit quite a bit now. One consideration which went into my picking the Ponds was that it is centrally located relative to my kids and to Newark Airport. I looked at Penns Woods and one in Needham, Massachusetts and a high rise CCRC in Connecticut."

When I asked her how she felt about living in a community inhabited only by her age peers, she answered,

"Age homogeneity is no problem for me because I prepared for it well in advance. But I was surprised by the number of canes, walkers, wheelchairs, electric carts etc. which didn't seem to be here during my visits. Hearing and sight problems result in many 'fantasy' conversational interchanges which are almost Kafkaesque. I am also surprised by the number of W.A.S.P.'s [i.e. White Anglo Saxon Protestants] "

Mrs. Harrison was unhappy with what she called the "forced formality" of the "dining event", and was "somewhat turned off" by the "seemingly irrelevant unwritten protocols of the place" such as calling neighbors on the phone rather than just knocking on the door. She told me that I had been "lucky" to not have violated this in my approaches to residents. And when I probed her about the opportunities for intellectual stimulation she said,

126

"They are lacking. I wanted to audit a course at [the nearby Ivy League university] but I decided it would be unfair to the professor and it would be hard to get there since courses are late in the day and I don't drive any more than I have to. I do take the bus to New York City once a week though. A friend suggested we organize courses for ourselves through the community college, but I am not sure I have the energy.

There seems to be a shortage of volunteers for the committees because I have already been asked to edit the Ponds Ponder. I feel that this is a problem with the older average age and infirmity of the residents. I want to be as active in the community as my physical condition will let me, but I am sensitive to the fact that I am still 'the new kid on the block'."

Mrs. Harrison was right in the center of the most aggressively involved faction of the New Turks. Among the most prominent in the group were her old friend Bessie Bancroft (an "old money" heiress and world adventuress who was also a thoroughly gracious lady) and Emmy Kolber (the exuberant, well traveled widow of a preeminent *New York Times* editor) in addition to her mentor Ellie Barnes who was a virtual renaissance woman.

I was taken with Mrs. Harrison and her vivacious coterie of accomplished friends. And because they, in turn, were interested in my research, I received a lot of useful advice for its implementation as well as many unique insights into this community.

Carl and Binkie Saunders, among others, strongly urged me to interview **Desmond South**, who they felt to be a good example of a successful adjustment to the CCRC life style. Calling Desmond South exuberant is a little like calling a category 5 hurricane a brisk wind. He not only wanted to see me, he wanted to see me "as soon as you can possibly fit me in". Mr. South was still a major force in the publishing world. He had also been, over the years, an officer or trustee of 27 boards associated with UNICEF, with UNESCO and with various international organizations involved with Asian cultural affairs.

Well into his late 80's, he still commuted once a week to his office in New York (before a recent hip replacement, he had commuted twice a week to two different New York offices!). Mr. South had two daughters who were equally accomplished and about whom he talked incessantly, with great and obvious pride. In fact, as soon as I arrived at his apartment, he wanted me to know about his daughters, before we got into anything else. He informed me,

> "I have two daughters, 51 and 54, who are both are doing their Ph.D.'s. One is at Columbia, majoring in American History and one is at Harvard. The one at Columbia used to be the head of a major psychiatric facility on the Hudson, so she is undergoing a complete career change. So what you're doing is fully legitimated."

Mr. South was anxious for me to know how well he had adapted to his current life style:

> "I came here five years ago, mainly so as not to be a burden to my two daughters. My adjustment was instantaneous, even though I left a large home and had to dispose of my 2,000 book collection of publishing history and graphic arts [he told me he gave these to the New York Public Library and to his alma mater, Princeton] and even though I loved both gardening and cooking. I have cooked ever since my sister got a kitchen with an oil-fired stove when I was nine years old.

128

I wanted to sign up without even looking at the place, but my daughters forced me to look. When I was down here looking and they called, they asked me if I had looked at the health facilities, and I said, 'no, but the pecan pie was excellent'."

And as for the gardening and cooking, he had found a way. He told me,

"I cook both my breakfast, after my 6 a.m. mile walk, and my lunch. And I have about 16 tomato plants which I got permission to plant instead of flowers. I grow the Ramapo tomatoes because the Rutgers tomatoes get the blight."

Mr. South proceeded to tell a few of the things he liked about the Ponds:

"I like the unique Ponds protocols in general, and I am particularly fond of the one hour, 4:45 to 5:45, cocktail party. I go to two a week on the average and I have some of my own; with exactly six people including myself. And I like the fact that everyone shakes hands and says 'good night' after dinner."

And he informed me of some of the economic benefits.

"There are some practical advantages to living in a place like this too. A certain portion of everyone's monthly fees are deductible for IRS purposes, as medical insurance. This amounts to 10 thousand dollars a year for me. As far as New Jersey is concerned, the Ponds residence can be treated – for tax deduction of real estate taxes - as if it is owned. I don't think that is true for federal taxes though, and some who are treating it that way may eventually get burned. Residents who don't enter the nursing facility until at least two years after they come here get a minimum of 50% of their entrance fees back."

In spite of Mr. South's love of the Ponds, however, there was one thing he didn't like:

"My main complaint about the Ponds is the lack of Black residents. I have several prominent Black friends, including a Princeton professor and the President of [a major New York City University] who I feel would be good candidates, but I just can't get enough interest for them to try it. Some of the people in the community would take it badly, but there are enough 'nice' people so it would be successful."

I pressed him for some of his thoughts on the financial stability of the Ponds and about the future of the CCRC industry in general. Mr. South was well informed in this area and very forthcoming.

"Although some here feel they are in financial trouble and in danger of folding, I think they will be 'O.K.'. There is 98% occupancy now or 282 of the 291 apartments filled. I feel that there would be a substantial waiting list if people weren't having trouble selling their homes.

Two years ago they let people in who were too infirm, because of their financial problems. But the new crowd is much better; they are a younger crowd. Although I don't feel age is a valid criterion for rejection. Regarding trends in the CCRC industry in general, I think there will be a boom, and big corporations are getting into it."

I asked Mr. South for the names of some others I should talk to. He gave me not only the names, but also brief editorial comments to go along with each:

> "You should see Amber Wentworth. She is living in sin with Hal Roth, who is chairman of the Greenhouse Committee and a pain in the butt. And Vanessa Kerry, the editor of *The Ponder*. And Gretta Born, whose husband was the head of [big name] Publishing and who has some interesting perspectives on the place.
>
> There are also some interesting people who hang out together who are associated in ways we are not sure of [my take is that these individuals, whose names I never learned, were not married but were living together]."

Mr. South was fascinated by the fact that my wife is from the Philippines. He had traveled extensively throughout Asia, both for pleasure and because of his international trusteeships, and he seemed to love the Philippines and the Filippinos. He told me of his experiences in the Far East, and before I left he insisted that I accept, as a gift for my wife, a beautifully photographed coffee table book on Philippine cuisine.

I have to admit that I was charmed by the gracious Mr. South. I include him in my New Turks category, because, unlike the "group" discussed in the following chapter (the group which I have designated as "The True Guests"), although he thoroughly enjoyed the amenities and the ambiance of the Ponds, he was also very much involved with its governance and very much concerned about its well being.

It was right in character for **Rosalie Gardiner**. Having just spent five weeks recovering from a broken pelvis, she was in the process of exploring the potential of music therapy for those confined to the nursing care unit; "touching them so that something sparks", as she put it. She had been a music teacher for many years, and her former husband was both a teacher and a concert pianist.

Mrs. Gardiner had been at the Ponds for less than a year when I first met her at the suggestion of Flow Harrison, a friend and mentor. She had born a heavy burden as the primary care giver to several family members prior to coming here. She told me,

> "Both my mother and my mother-in-law – who was no great friend, but who I took in to allay my husband's guilt and make my marriage work better – lived in my home in succession. I came to the Ponds after researching Monte Vista a year and a half ago. The previous five years were involved with taking care of my husband [a second marriage she informed me] who had cancer. The last two years were very difficult, but good years."

She seemed close to tears at this point, but continued her story.

> "I had a real problem gaining the confidence of my husband's son who was then four and a half. The boy had a lot of love, between his father and his aunt (who took him every weekend) and his grand-mother, and he was not manifesting any real love for me. I broke out in hives with no apparent allergy, and my doctor told me to 'search my soul' for something that was bothering me.
>
> Because we lived in a small New York City apart-ment and my husband and my son-in-law were always home when I was, I walked through Central Park to search my soul. And I figured out that the

boy didn't love me, I hadn't 'captured' him. I decided to relax and leave it to fate, and one night he asked me to give him a bath, which he considered a privilege for the 'lucky giver'. And he told me, 'I can see why my Daddy loves you.' We were all right with each other after that."

Mrs. Gardiner told me that she was happy with the Ponds. She had a childhood friend here, and two other people she knew before coming. She told me,

"I have made a nice group of friends here, and I believe we see each other as surrogate family because we are all in the same set of circumstances. What I like about the place is the impressive variety of backgrounds here and that people are willing to talk about themselves. What I don't like is that fact that so many are so old. Even though they have impressive backgrounds, they are losing their faculties or losing their desire to exert the energy necessary to show their talents."

She then proceeded to give me examples of what she meant.

"We tried to form a sing-along and found that many had lost their former abilities and needed real drilling. Yet more than half were never able to make it to the rehearsals. And Jeanne Sandler and I came up with the idea of the Ponds residents' lecture series, which has not been very successful because of the lack of interest on the part of the residents and the lack of interested speakers. Even Jeanne, who gave two great lectures on literature, couldn't hold their interest because of her failing voice. Most of these people are retired and don't care any longer to discipline themselves to teach."

When she discussed with me her adjustment to her own move to the Ponds, she also offered her philosophy as to what is necessary for one's successful transition to the CCRC life style:

> "Moving was very traumatic for me in terms of leaving old friends and in terms of disposing of things due to the much more limited space. I was the first in my group to do it, and they disapproved of what I was doing. In my mind there is a 'window of opportunity' for the move in terms of age. You can't be too old to expend energy, but you have to be old enough so that the sacrifices in terms of former life style are offset by the necessity of the supportive environment.

> Those who come with negative attitudes don't last very long. I now look at old friends from the standpoint of whether on not they would do well at the Ponds or an equivalent CCRC. Some have no family at all, or family who don't see them, and those definitely should be here where they have a substitute family.

> Most people here are in the same boat and are empathetic. I personally helped two people acclimate to the place by having dinner every night with them for a week and introducing them to people, activities, protocol etc."

And when I asked her about the presence of statuses within the resident body, she told me,

> "They definitely exist here and are emphasized by the dichotomy between singles and couples; the same as in society at large. This is at least partially attributable to the fact that single people feel like

134

fifth wheels in the presence of couples, and they disseminate that feeling to others."

Mrs. Gardiner was a warm and friendly lady and a good informant. She more or less typified the level of concern for and involvement with the community which characterized those individuals who I have designed as the New Turks.

But beyond that, this charming lady provided for me many valuable insights into how the "natives" (both her resident peer group and her cohort group in general) see themselves and their place within the larger society. I am most grateful to her for helping me with this critical perspective of my research.

Emmy Kolber's apartment was filled with the beautiful Japanese antiques she had collected over the years she had lived in Japan with two successive husbands, both now deceased. She was good friends with both Flow Harrison and Rosalie Gardiner.

In fact, it was Mrs. Harrison who had strongly urged me to interview Mrs. Kolber; that referral immediately earned me Mrs. K's confidence, and quickly precipitated my first invitation to her apartment. With virtually no prodding from me, this delightful woman filled me in on the high points of her pre-Ponds background. She told me,

> "I was born in Mountain View, New Jersey, and spent most of my childhood there. I graduated from Bennington College with a degree in English in 1924. My first husband was a reporter for AP - he was an aggressive rival of the 'flamboyant' John Howard of Scripps Howard and their UP - who volunteered for a three year tour of duty in Japan in 1925.

135

I later returned for a period of nine years with the MacArthur occupation with my second husband who was a reporter with a by-line for *The Washington Post*. I myself was a freelance writer for a Japanese daily. I also taught weaving classes to the Japanese and, in turn, I took courses in flower arranging and tea service."

She told me about some of the creative ways in which her second husband - who apparently taught English to Japanese youngsters while he was in Japan - conveyed visual images of objects and events to his students. For example, an exploding volcano:

"...great rocks flew from the under to the up with smoke from their behinds."

Mrs. Kolber's fascination with the Japanese continued after her return to New York in the early 1950's. She told me that,

"While living in an apartment in the 60's on the East Side of Manhattan, I was active in various Japanese organizations including the Japan Society; I was a founder of the New York Chapter of that organization. Also, as an independent travel agent, I booked 10 very profitable tours to Japan."

Mrs. Kolber like her good friends Flow Harrison (Mrs. K's half sister was a classmate of Mrs. Harrison) and Rosalie Gardiner, was a long time member of the League of Women Voters. It seemed that she agreed with her friends, though, that the League was not active enough in forcing state legislation regarding matters of concern to the elderly such as living wills. Regarding her tenure at the ponds, Mrs. Kolber told me,

"I have been here for more than ten years, I came in 1978. I was told about the place by another resident who was the daughter of my first husband's employer in Japan and who is from a very prominent family who made their name in yarn. It was perfect for me in terms of location because my daughter, my only child, lives in Trenton and my sister is a permanent resident of the nursing care unit.

The physical transition wasn't bad for me, moving from a New York apartment, but I miss young people, and I am aware of a certain falloff in propriety - relative to the 'old days' - associated with dinner dress ."

When I questioned her about it, she admitted she had no problems with the changes which had occurred at the Ponds over the course of her residency. She also confessed to a liberal past and to an "itch" to pursue her writing.

"I accept change. Increased informality, increased costs, an aging population – these are reflective of what is happening in society at large. I did like the way things were being run when Minerva Beasley was editor of *The Ponder* though, Minerva is a great friend. The guts are cut out of some of the submissions now, but I am thinking of submitting something about your research.

I would also like to publish something about my life experiences; in the form of an autobiography maybe. I am a bit of a feminist actually. I belonged to a number of suffragist organizations when I was much younger, and I wore a black tie when women first lost the vote."

When I addressed the issue of ethnic biases, particularly anti-Semitism, at the Ponds, she admitted that they were definitely there.

"There is a real presence of anti-Semitism in this community. I won't get into specific examples though. I greatly admire some of our Jewish residents. I love Flora Mortenson's [the widow of an extremely prominent Ivy League professor of Sociology] spunk. But I am a little put off by Dr. Brontman's forced expression of Jewishness and its accomplishments on the one hand and her apologist attitudes toward it on the other."

But what was really a passionate issue for Mrs. Kolber was what she referred to as the "non-status" of the elderly:

"We are really missing a great resource in our elderly. As we age as a society we will see forced changes in these attitudes; as the baby boomers themselves reach old age. I want to stay in touch with you and see your research."

And stay in touch we did. I had lunch and dinner with Mrs. Kolber and "the girls" on more than one occasion, and she and I conversed regularly, sometimes almost daily. She really was interested in what I was doing, and was always suggesting additional resources for me to explore. She seemed to appreciate my interest in the problems of the elderly, and I, in turn, was fascinated listening to the details of the rich and interesting life of this charming and worldly lady.

Chapter Eight

The Real Guests

Geraldine Majors, at the age of 95, had been a resident of the Ponds for 20 years when I met her. She was a straight-shooting, feisty old gal, but she was also a loner, who had never really joined in the same spirit of community that many of the residents from the other 'groups' had. Mrs. Majors had moved here at the age of 75 with her husband, since deceased, who had been a successful New York City attorney.

She was the only child of wealthy parents who had owned a beautiful city home in the Bronx - when living there was 'fashionable' - and a large country estate in upstate New York. She was schooled in New York City at an elite college preparatory school and a premier art college. Her mother felt that her daughter was a "born artist", so, even though Mrs. Majors had wanted to be a business woman, she had pursued her art to keep peace in the family. She told me,

> "I came to the Ponds after I looked at the place with a good friend. My friend came right away, but I resisted because I didn't want to give up the cat I loved. Eventually I had to have my cat put away because I was pressured by the Ponds to make the move. I liked it because I never got off home territory and I didn't feel like I was in prison; although I would have preferred to be in Connecti-cut.
>
> At first I went back and forth to New York a lot and elsewhere. There has always been an extraordinarily intelligent group of residents here. This is a splen-did place to finish off your final years."

When I queried her about it, Mrs. Majors didn't seem to have the same fond memories of the so called "golden years" as others in her 'group' had.

> "I was neither married [her husband was deceased] nor on the make for a man, and now that I am on the old side of it I don't want cocktails and all that stuff."

She made no bones about certain of her ethnic biases either,

> "There are a lot of Central Europeans here. What do you think will happen when they let Blacks and the like in here? I don't like them, don't ya see, but I am interested in them [i.e. the 'Central Europeans'] and I talk to them. People are just as interesting as reading. I have dinner occasionally with my neighbor Dr. Loren Aczell from Budapest."

One of Mrs. Major's quandaries as a loner, however, was the lack of a formal intermediate care unit at the Ponds. Although she didn't want a companion, she didn't want to end up permanently in the nursing unit either. But she wasn't in the least bit afraid of the prospect of her death, in fact she welcomed it and she had some unique ideas about it. She was happy to discuss these with me.

> "I am into metaphysics. I wonder if some of the others you have talked to are also interested in this sort of thing? I believe in reincarnation. We are constantly evolving toward something better, don't ya see, and our co-residents are all in various stages of evolution, and the proof of this is the notion that we have sometimes of already knowing someone who we have not met in this life. The meeting was in a former life. I have tried this out with mystics."

In spite of this, however, she was also a confirmed Episcopalian who attended Presbyterian services (she had no workable access to Episcopal services). When I asked Mrs. Majors if there was anything that she had missed in her life, she told me,

"I don't miss not having a brilliant career, and I had a happy marriage. I wanted to travel more after my husband died though. I kept procrastinating. I didn't realize that old age would creep up so fast and limit me. I believe that with my reincarnation though, I will eventually do, be and see everything. The down side now is that I am sick of my old body. But death isn't talked about here, don't ya see."

Mrs. Majors seemed to be focused on the other side of her own demise. She was not involved with other Ponds residents socially, and she was not interested in any of the facility's activities. She had no old friends anymore and, apparently, no immediate family. Her only interest in the welfare of the community involved its continued ability to provide her with food and lodging until she was reincarnated into her next life.

Unlike the New Turks, most of whom viewed life at the Ponds as a sort of "second chance", Mrs. Majors looked upon it merely as the prelude to her final life passage. Unlike the Village Elders, she wanted no part in the governance of the place, in spite of her lengthy tenure, and, unlike even her fellow "Real Guests", she had no interest in seeking a camaraderie with her fellow residents.

Although I never "formally" interviewed **Harvey** and **Merin Coulter** during my residency at the Ponds, I saw them frequently in the common areas of the facility, and we always stopped to chat, usually at length. As mentioned in an earlier chapter, Mr. Coulter had a fascination with the Ponds wildlife, but very little interest in talking about his former role as the head of research for a huge communications conglomerate.

If one were to hear the Coulters' running commentary about life at the Ponds one would think that they were either reviewing a resort hotel for a travel magazine or that they had been involuntarily committed to a low security prison:

"...it is an institution...the food is very good considering the number cooked for, but not great. You have to check out if you leave over night, and I don't like the electric carts because I think that some of the people are too old to drive, or at least don't have good enough eyesight. We both have all of our physical faculties; we don't need canes or electric carts, and we don't need the nursing facility yet. We have our escapes though; a condo near Daytona Beach."

When I mentioned the Ponds-sponsored excursions run by Marcie Jean Franklin, the facility's Director of Resident Activities, Mr. Coulter told me,

"Marcie Jean Franklin, because of the size of the Ponds' limo, only deals in groups of several people for most of the trips, events and so on. The groups who go are either in some sort of clique connected to her mother, who is a resident, or are too small to really be of importance to the resident community at large. And the France trip this fall is not sponsored by the Ponds."

The Coulters had lived in Princeton, New Jersey and in California during Mr. Coulter's career with the communications conglomerate. Their son, who they told me is "very independent", is doing his Ph.D. in philosophy in Colorado. Mrs. Coulter - a very energetic woman with a keen wit and a

degree from the University of Pennsylvania (class of 1931) –
always did most of the talking. They had been residents of
the Ponds for one year at this point. In spite of what she had
said earlier though, she admitted,

> "We know we really do need a place like this. We
> were considering Penns Wood, but a friend told us
> it was just like this place. All of the better ones are
> pretty much alike. The degree of satisfaction with
> this lifestyle though, is directly correlated to what
> you did and the way you lived before you got here,
> which is not correlated to the amount of wealth;
> everyone here has above average wealth to be here.
> If people were active and outgoing, they are proba-
> bly much more unhappy with the limitations of both
> the place and with their own bodies."

When I complemented Mrs. Coulter on her wonderful sense
of humor, she replied,

> "A sense of humor is one of the things that keeps
> you going; it is the manifestation of a positive
> attitude. It has worked for me. I had two close
> brushes with death, including lymphosarcoma, and
> came out fine. I don't deny that old age takes its
> toll, however.
>
> I am worried about Harvey's driving because his
> reactions aren't as fast as they used to be. But, on
> the other hand, he walks so fast that I won't walk
> with him, and he swims 25 or thirty laps in the
> swimming pool every day."

And then, as if to further certify her reputation for her sense
of humor, she told me a very funny story:

"There was an old man who used to keep all of his money in his mattress because he wanted to take it with him. He made his wife promise to bury it with him when he died. After he finally did die, their friends asked the wife if she actually buried all of his money with him. She said 'yes', she had put all of his money in the bank and then wrote a check on the account and put it in the coffin."

The Coulters owned a condominium in Florida where they spent most of each winter. Although the Ponds was their "official" residence for IRS and other business purposes, they looked on it merely as a second residence at a fashionable address, not as their permanent home base or as their "community". As such, they were interested in the good food, the dependable maintenance of the physical plant, and in the social and recreational possibilities.

They were not, on the other hand, interested in how the place worked or in any of its political intrigue. And they had no real desire to participate on any of the Ponds resident committees. "Living" at the Ponds also made good business sense to the Coulters in terms of their medical needs and their probable future use of the facility's nursing care, both of which were contractually guaranteed to them as Ponds residents.

Running into the Coulters regularly was one of the highpoints of my research at the Ponds. As Mrs. Coulter became more comfortable with me, she confided many of the little details of her pre-Ponds life, such as the time a teacher at college threw her in the pool and about how her father, who was a druggist, insisted that she talk to the customers even if she didn't know them. And Mr. Coulter was very easy to engage in conversation as long as the conversation involved either a critique of the Ponds or animals and nature.

Even though this interesting couple had not been fully "socialized" into the Ponds *qua* community, they seemed to really enjoy partaking of its amenities; much as one might enjoy the comforts of a luxury vacation destination.

I think that it was Carl Saunders who suggested that I talk to the Nortons. He felt that they had a number of unique observations pertaining to the CCRC adjustment process which might be of interest to me. I phoned **Dr. Ray Norton**, introduced myself and arranged to meet with him at his apartment.

Once there, I filled in Dr. Norton (Mrs. Norton, "Millie", was out doing the laundry) on the nature and intent of my research. Then I asked him why he had decided to move to a CCRC and to the Ponds in particular. He said that,

> "With no immediate family of my own, my primary concern is medical care. We lived in a lovely big home in Bernardsville. After an attorney friend in New York recommended the Ponds to us, we put our names on a waiting list, but turned it down the first time because we wanted to have a big celebration of our 50th anniversary.
>
> The second time we accepted, because we were afraid that if we turned it down we would not be able to get in when we needed it. We have friends here from Sea Island Georgia, where we have a vacation condo [one of their friends is Nellie Steiger]. We also have friends from Franklin Lakes who have since moved here."

Dr. Norton was the chairman of the 65th reunion of his graduating class at the nearby Ivy League University. Planning for this occasion, now a month away, had taken an entire year; he was obviously very proud of the school and of the effort he had put in to organizing the reunion. The

145

proximity of the University to the Ponds was another primary factor in his decision to move here. As to how he felt about the greatly reduced amount of living space, he told me,

"In terms of adjusting to the more limited space, we were given forms depicting the exact specifications of each of the areas of the apartment, and cutouts for furniture, so we could decide exactly what pieces we could take. I adjusted to college all right. I adjusted to the Navy all right. I adjusted to medical school all right. So what is one more adjustment?

The view from the back reminds us very much of the view from our back yard in Bernardsville; the slate terrace, the brick wall, etc. I joined in participating in a number of sports right away to get to know more people."

And as to the logistics of vacating his former large home he told me,

"We had a professional team of ladies do a house sale. We were surprised at how much of the stuff went, at what price and how fast. They're a lot of people who fancy old stuff; out of date stuff."

At this point he made an unconnected observation as to how the elderly seem to re-connect to nature:

"I feel that elderly people, no matter what their profession and how far it removed them from contact with nature, want to somehow return to 'mother earth'."

I had been told by Mr. Saunders that Dr. Norton had written at least one article for *The Ponder*. When I asked him about it, he informed me,

"I have written several articles for them, but not lately. The one I wrote lately was about sports, because that is what they asked me to write about. But they said it was too long, and they edited out the part I felt was most critical, about how newcomers begin sports here. I didn't bother to revise it. I don't care much for the new editor."

Mrs. Norton came in through the back door with her finished laundry. I learned that she had an advanced degree in clinical psychology, and had worked on the board of trustees at a hospital in West Orange, New Jersey. When I asked them if they felt there was any sort of a deficit of intellectual stimulation at the Ponds, as proposed to me by Jeanne Sandler, Mrs. Norton said she could not understand how that could be given the wide professional diversity of the resident body. It was obvious to me that it was a non-issue with both of them, so I didn't bother to pursue it any further.

I have placed Dr. and Mrs. Norton in my "Guest" category because of the manner in which they "used" the facility and the way in which they seemed to perceive it. They came to the Ponds already knowing other residents in a social context, and additional friends followed them there shortly.

The Nortons fully utilized the amenities of the place, but were uninvolved in its resident committees, in its politics, or in its cohesion as a community. And they spent a part of each year at a second residence, where they continued to maintain the continuity of their primary/former friendship group.

Samuel Johnson was a warm, friendly man with a total lack of pretension. Immediately on entering his apartment for our first of several meetings, he asked me to call him "Sam". He told me that he had been an accountant during most of his working years, and had retired as a senior partner of one of the (then) big 8 accounting firms. Mr. Johnson had also been Chairman of the board of [the prestigious college preparatory school in Hightown], and was currently active on the Board of Directors of Holland American lines. Prior to entering the Ponds, he had resided at an assisted care facility. He told me,

"After many years as a resident of Short Hills, New Jersey, I moved to Rose Commons. I moved to the Ponds this past April after the death of my wife. At Rose Commons you do all of your own cooking and internal maintenance and you contract privately for everything else including medical care. We had some medical care available on premises, but not total care or a resident physician."

Mr. Johnson was very proud of his degree from Princeton University, but he was even prouder of his two daughters.

"Both of my daughters graduated from Barnard College. When they went there, Barnard was very hard to get into. My oldest daughter has a Ph.D. in education, and I have a granddaughter who is a student at Williams."

When I asked him about his adjustment to the CCRC life style, he told me,

"My continued involvement with my work and with my university helped me adjust to this type of community in terms of less space, age homogeneity and so on. I like not having to worry about health care, food etc., and I love the ambiance of this place.

People do get insular though. They get wrapped in a cacoon, in their own little world; it's easy to do. But with me, my family is number one. The family is the basic unit of all civilization. My daughters were very strong for me and helped me through the hard times."

Mr. Johnson ended our interview at that point, because he was expecting his daughter to pick him up. He told me that he was fascinated by my "project" and that he had thoroughly enjoyed our talk. He also asked me to have dinner with him the following week. We did continue to see each other off and on throughout the balance of my stay at the Ponds.

Mr. Johnson, it seemed, liked the convenience of the Ponds, the medical security that it provided for him and its amenities. When he thought of "home" though, he visualized his two daughters and their families and his deceased wife. For him, the notion of "community" conjured up reminiscences of Princeton and of Short Hills, not identification with the Ponds.

I got a call in my room one evening from a resident named **Ed Geller**. He asked me if we could talk for about ten minutes and then asked me if it should be my place or his. It turned out that two of the floor staff - Marcella Evans and Linda Kolber - had suggested that he should talk to me (I had also left a message to call on his answering machine).

He called, he told me, because he wanted to "go on record", so to speak, as to his rationale for choosing the CCRC life style.

"Rachael [i.e. Mrs. Geller, his wife] and I have been here for about four years, but we have been planning to come to a retirement community, in terms of 'buying into the concept' for18 years; since I was

149

60. I am still active as an independent contractor in the business of planning office furniture needs. I used to have my own company named Boston Desks. I am also active on four boards of directors, I do consulting work and I give lectures."

Their interest in the retirement community concept arose from the difficult times they had experienced taking care of their own aging parents. He said,

"We didn't want to impose those problems on our four children. Two of our children live close by in Toms River, New Jersey. Then there is one in Washington. D.C. and one in Arizona. Our son who lives in Arizona is the head master of a private school which specializes in children with difficulties.

Also, I had a scare when Rachael fell and broke her knee and I had to drive through a bad part of town in the middle of the night to get her to the hospital. I know I wouldn't want her doing that if the situation were reversed. So, the in-house medical care is a big factor for us. We came here three months after her accident, even though they told us there was a five year waiting list."

He continued with his praise of the Ponds:

"We like everything about the place, from the staff to the activities available. I build furniture from kits at the shop with the help of Hal Roth, who knows how to maintain all of the tools. Hal does magnificent woodworking. He is the one who found the shop and renovated it for use by the residents.

We like the security, and we like the ease of entertaining. We thought we would cook in our apartment, but we soon found the joys of the dining room. I think it's great taking someone to dinner, not paying because it is part of our monthly fee, and then being thanked as if we entertained!"

There was only one negative comment about the Ponds during my interview. Mrs. Geller, it turned out, had some problems with what she perceived as a certain "type" of resident:

"We spend July and August in our condo at the shore. You have to get away; being around all of these old people gets to you sometimes. Many of the ones coming now don't contribute, and they quickly take up a bed in the nursing care unit."

Mr. Geller was anxious to get more of his fellow Colby alumnae to come to the Ponds. In pursuit of that goal, he told me.

"I have been particularly active in the marketing campaign. I sent our pictures along with some advertising materials about the place to the weekly Colby magazine, and I have answered questions from Colby alumnae. I have also contacted friends personally, particularly at the 55th annual reunion this year."

The Gellers were the most organized residents I encountered, in terms of their retirement plans. They had decided 14 years before they actually moved to the Ponds that the CCRC was their retirement choice. And their attitude toward the exact timing of the move had been, more or less,

"...when the time is right we will know it. We looked to the Ponds as a more comfortable place - given our stage of life - in which to continue our former life style with former friends, or at least with our social peers. We try to utilize everything the place has to offer, to the fullest, but we have no intentions of giving up our alternate vacation residence."

Mr. Geller, far from isolating himself in this self-contained community, remained totally involved with his professional career. The Ponds was the Geller's place of residence, but they were no more involved with its "workings" as a self-contained social entity than any commuter might be with his or her suburban 'bedroom' community.

Chapter Nine

The Outliers

A significant minority of Ponds residents didn't, as one might suspect, fit neatly (or at all) into any of the "categories" of residents discussed in the previous four chapters. My use of the term "Outliers" is not meant to infer that the members of the group that I have so designated were social mavericks. Most, however, were either not openly welcomed into any of the community's social groups, or they themselves had elected not to join them.

Even if these non participants behaved somewhat eccentrically vis-a-vis the social "norms" of the resident body which had evolved at the Ponds over the years, however, they were by no means "troublemakers" when it came to abiding by the "official" rules of the place; exactly the opposite in most cases. Like everyone else at the Ponds, these individuals were just interesting people who, voluntarily or not, "marched to different drummers."

And easily the premier example of the category was my next door neighbor, the inimical **Helene Cousins**. At 97 (per the Ponds medical records), Mrs. Cousins was a true eccentric, still holding on to a lust for life. I made my first contact with her one evening when, after wandering out of her back door, she came over and pressed her face against my back window and gave me a very startled look. I opened my back door and went outside to introduce myself . She proceeded to tell me in breathless, unconnected phrases,

> "I usually don't snoop. This used to be Mrs. Newman's apartment, how long have you been here?"

[Jeannie Seaver, her private aid and companion, told me later that Mrs. C. was always complaining that her back door didn't work, because she was always trying to get in my back door, thinking it was hers.] And she continued, as if we already great friends,

> "I want you to join me for a drink some evening, although not tonight. I have pretty much everything to drink; rum, whiskey, beer – that's my son in law's favorite – and Dubonet, which I drink because it's simple. I am 94, and I am going blind. There is something wrong with every one of my flowers here. Last year a man took care of them. Next year my daughter will help me with them."

Even though I explained who I was and what I was doing there, I am convinced that she never really understood my mission at the Ponds. That didn't really matter much though, because we got along fine with each other.

I was introduced to Jeanne Seaver, Mrs. Cousins' private aid and companion, in the employee cafeteria one morning when I was having breakfast with several of the floor staff. My conversation with this group focused primarily, as was often the case, on their problems with their respective employers. During that meal, and in subsequent conversations I had with Jeannie, she conveyed another side to Mrs. Cousins' cute "quirkiness":

> "She is always feeling sorry for herself. Her complaints are so trivial relative to the real world. She buys expensive dresses – loves to spend money – even though there is no point in it. And she drinks 4-5 bottles of Dubonet a week. She thinks she can do some things like drive an electric cart – even though she really can't – because she is unwilling to accept the reality of her limitations."

According to Jeannie, in spite of her apparent joy for living, Mrs. Cousins was also preparing herself for her own demise:

"Mrs. Cousins has all of the accessories she wants to be buried in chosen and set aside. She loses her jewelry all the time though. She has been bugging me to buy her a custom-tailored black velvet dress in town specifically for the viewing prior to her cremation and the scattering of her ashes at sea among the racing sailboats. It gives me the creeps, and I won't buy the dress because it might be a bad omen in terms of signaling her death."

But then, on a more sympathetic note, she told me,

"She is having a cocktail party at 6 tonight to celebrate her birthday. I can't wait to dress her up."

I can vouch for Mrs. Cousins' love for her Dubonet, because I often saw the empty bottles next to her front door waiting to be recycled. She frequently had male visitors in for cocktails (Jeannie informed me that Mrs. Cousins's daughter wouldn't let Mrs. C see her current boy friend anymore). Another area of friction between Jeannie and her employer involved Jeannie's desire to obtain her certification as a medical aid.

One afternoon while I was in my apartment typing notes and arranging resident interviews, I overheard Jeannie responding to what seemed to be Mrs. Cousins' concern that her companion was leaving her:

"I am not leaving you, I'm just going for two days a week for six weeks to take nurses aid courses."

I didn't hear Mrs. Cousins' response to this, but, judging by what I heard next from Jeannie, it wasn't very supportive.

"I am smarter than you think I am. I could pass the certification with no problem, I just want to learn more about certain areas like bathing someone in bed. And just because I am certified doesn't mean I will ask for $15 an hour. I like you, and I would work for you at the same rate."

My cocktail date with Mrs. Cousins never materialized, and my acquaintance with this unique lady never included a one on one interview. We did bump into each other fairly frequently in the hallway outside of our respective residences though, and our brief conversational exchanges were always cordial and, well, different. Mrs. Cousins' reputation as one of the local "characters" kept administrative and floor staff buzzing with stories of her exploits, and Jeannie was a never ending source of antidotes regarding her employer.

Evelyne McAllister, at the age of 82, was still, at heart, a New Yorker. She had come to the Ponds at the insistence of her brother, who lived in nearby Highville, after an unusually traumatic mugging near her Riverside Drive apartment. She was immediately taken under the wing of Dr. Merton, who was trying to help her adjust to these unfamiliar surroundings, to get over her hurt, and to make new friends.

Dr. Merton, a fellow artist, had been asked, I was told, to have dinner with Mrs. McAllister when she first arrived. They had quickly become good friends. But, according to Mrs. Gardiner who urged me to meet Mrs. McAllister, adjustment was an uphill battle for Mrs. M. Mrs.Gardiner told me,

> "She is a very interesting person; a writer and an artist. But she is not adjusting. She is not interested in writing, and she thinks people here stuffy. She misses the City. She would enjoy talking to you because you are involved there."

Using Mrs. Gardiner as my referral, I set up my first of two meetings with Mrs. McAllister. Her apartment was very dark because there was no overhead light at all, and none of the table lamps were on. I sat on the couch facing the slider

156

doors to her terrace, and she sat on an easy chair across from me. When I asked her if she would mind telling me a little about herself, she gave a compact but comprehensive (and very poignant) summary of her background:

> "I was born in Yokahama, Japan of Dutch parents, and lived there until the age of 12 when my parents moved to the States. I received my BA from the Yale School of Fine Arts. I later also studied at Barnard College, at the Art Student's League, and with a Zen Master in Japan, where I met my husband, who was a foreign service major.
>
> My specialty is modernist art using woodcuts and pastels. I loved to play the piano as a child, but I sensed that I was only mediocre at it, and I stopped playing after my mother, shortly before taking her own life, requested that I play my whole repertoire for her.
>
> Music and reading are my two greatest joys now, however. I spend a lot of time listening to music and lying down reading book after book. And since I lost the sight of one eye I spend a lot of time raising plants [in the Ponds greenhouse] and writing my memoirs for my children."

In fact, Mrs. McAllister is an extremely accomplished and nationally recognized artist. I was told by Dr. Merton that her works had been exhibited in, among other places, The Brooklyn Museum, the Society of Washington Printmakers, the Philadelphia Print Club and the Corcoran Gallery of Art. The Library of Congress and the U.S. Information Agency had purchased several pieces of her art for display in U.S. embassies abroad.

157

She was also asked to exhibit 150 of her prints at the Hilton Printmakers Show in New York City shortly before our first meeting. She continued her life story:

> "I also lived in Germany for 7 years during the post WWII reconstruction where my husband was a diplomat and an assistant to the U.S. State Department. I, myself, helped to rebuild the artistic 'soul' of Germany by organizing in Bonn an exhibition of the work of 112 artists who had been persecuted by Hitler.
>
> These were the most interesting, useful and rewarding, but also the saddest years of my life. When I returned to the States I lived in Westchester County where I sent three daughters to the public schools."

And regarding her life at the Ponds:

> "I have a real love-hate relationship with this place. It was very traumatic moving here from New York. But although I miss the vibrancy and culture of New York, I love the woods and the bucolic views from my apartment. And I love the luxury and the quality of care I get here, and the Frank Lloyd Wright and Japanese inspired architecture.
>
> But I hate the dark corridors. They remind me of a mortuary to the point where I walk outside whenever I can. The best way to look at the Ponds is to pretend you are moving around in a surrealist picture…it is the theater of the absurd.
>
> What I fear the most is the loss of the 'giving element' of life. I have seen people here who have lost that. I want to continue to do and learn more and to stay interested. I initiated a group of five people here who read any kind of fictional and non-

fictional materials to each other. Last week I read the entire op-ed page of the *Times* to the group when it focused, with George Sick, on the Iran Contra Affair."

At the conclusion of our initial meeting, Mrs. McAllister asked me to join her for dinner the following week. During our dinner, she detailed the extent of the injuries she had received at the hands of the group of teen age muggers in New York. She told me that they had broken her arm, and that she had cracked all of her teeth when she had fallen. She was now forced to walk with a cane, and when she had fallen a second time at the Ponds she learned that she was going to have to have all of her teeth replaced.

In spite of all of the woman's physical pain, however, Mrs. M's main concern seemed to be that she was being sidetracked or "put out to pasture" in the old folks home. I believed that socialization to this sort of lifestyle was going to be extremely difficult for this accomplished, yet haunted lady of the world.

Residents of the Ponds nursing care unit were *de facto* "outliers" by circumstance, not by choice. As already discussed, those who were forced to live in the total care facility due to their deteriorating health, were pretty much forgotten (except by a small number of female volunteers) by those still living independently in their own apartments. I decided that my study of the Ponds would not be complete until I had gotten to know at least one of these individuals well.

Dr. Daria Learner was the nursing care resident most often recommended to me by the floor staff and by the administration, so I decided to grab the bull by the horns and make her acquaintance.

159

Dr. Learner, who had been at the Ponds for ten years, was 95 when I met her. She was obviously very happy to have a visitor, and, with her warm and friendly manner, she put me immediately at ease. When I asked her to tell me a little about herself, the words just flowed out of her.

It seemed that she wanted to tell me the story of her life. And, because I felt that she would make a good study for a life history (something I had not yet undertaken at the Ponds), I decided to forego my semi-structured interviewing strategy and to just listen to her story. What follows is a few of the highpoints of that story in her own words:

> "I received both my BA and my MA from the University of Chicago. I got my Ph.D. at New York University in aging studies. My thesis was: 'Family Adjustment in Aging: Grandmothers in the Home'.
>
> Before I got my college degrees though I taught English to World War I immigrants in British Columbia after receiving training from the Superintendent of Education in Regina. I got the job straight out of high school because my English pronunciation was overheard in a high school debate by the British Columbia Superintendent of Education.
>
> I had 26 students, and I had to ride over 20 miles to work in a horse and buggy. I had no notion of where the children came from, and did not know any of their languages, but I used many repetitions of simple objects such as a cup, while holding them and adding a verb such as 'down'. I also used the Berlitz method, which I had learned in a short course, for non-English speaking students.
>
> It was so cold in the winter that they had to close school; colder than Scandinavia. I made a good

friend with a lady from Iceland who spoke perfect English and later became a member of the Canadian Parliament. I got the job because my English was so good. My mother, who taught English would not allow me to speak bad English and she made me look up and learn new words every day."

Dr. Learner was having such a good time reminiscing about her past that I just let her ramble on.

"I was courted by two men at the same time at the University of Chicago and was made love to. By that I mean that we held hands and cuddled. I finally chose Herman Learner because when we were riding together one day we had a car accident where the baby being held by his mother was hurt and Herman immediately took the baby in his arms and told me to run to any door in the hospital and get an ambulance. My other suitor was more interested in the damage to our car. After our marriage we moved to Nyack."

She then told me about her children.

"I have three children – two boys and one girl – some grandchildren and two great grandchildren. I like the grandmother role because I can enjoy my grandchildren, seeing how they resemble the children, without the responsibility. My son, who was living in Phoenix, Arizona recently died of cancer.

My daughter in law drove all the way here to tell me, then she drove his ashes all the way to the church in Nyack, where he had lived the longest and where my family had some members buried. She didn't tell me that he was ill because there was nothing anyone could do, and she didn't want to make me miserable."

When she told this to me, Dr. Learner was obviously fighting to hold back her tears. She was squeezing my hand and asking God to make her strong (at this point I was asking God to make me strong too!). Then she relayed an incident which had taken place between her husband and her son:

"When he was a boy he hung out with the wrong crowd; a crowd that had robbed some stores. My husband had gotten tickets for the Yale-Harvard game, but he told my son that they weren't going to the game because the son wouldn't stop hanging out with that group of criminals.

My son asked his father why he wasn't going to the game; after all it was he, not his father, who was being punished. My husband told him that the son is part of the father, they are one in the same, and a consequence for one becomes a consequence for the other."

And then she told me about her husband's passing and the effect it had on his grandson. Dr. Learner had stayed at her daughter's house while her husband was in the hospital on his death bed.

"My grandson used to get out of bed against his mother's orders and go down stairs to talk to me. Later, I was the one also who had to tell him his grandfather was on his death bed and that he wouldn't see him again. When he visited me here he told me that he missed my funny stories and me kissing him good night. He told his mother, 'it isn't right for grandmother to be in an old age home'."

When I next saw Dr. Learner, about two weeks later, it was as if I had never left. She started right in on her reminiscences with series of new anecdotes (and frequent repetitions of things she had already told me) about her husband and other members of her family. One thread which seemed to run through all of their lives was their propensity to earn money.

> "When I met my husband the first thing I noticed was how big his feet were. I was startled, all I saw was feet. He had such big feet and hands that he had to buy his gloves at a special store. He also had to go to the better stores like Lord & Taylor for underwear. Herman was born in Portland, Maine. Grandpa Learner, Herman's father, was a sea captain form Norway; we visited him there. Herman won an award as Civil Engineer and went on to make a lot of money."

And about her own parents:

> "My family, the Harrisons, were all teachers or preachers. Father was a Ph.D. in chemistry. He was a big, quiet man who loved his children. He ended up making a lot of money in candy for Hersheys after first teaching and working for General Electric. My mother thought it was shameful for a Ph.D. to be a candy maker. She was a good teacher. She sent me to Webster whenever I didn't know or missed a word."

And then a much longer tale about her son and daughter in law:

> " My son and daughter in law met and fell in love in their senior year of high school. When they told us that they were going to get married, we told them that since he was going to Colorado and she was

163

going to St. Lukes in New York to study nursing, they should consider the possibility that their love might not last. They should do whatever they could to lessen the pain of breaking it off.

Well, they took most of our advice; when she was finished and he had one more year, they got married in Nyack, and then moved to Boulder. Then he gets the idea of making crystal commercially and gets backing from two older men. They built their first plant near Dallas, and then more plants, and he became rich and they moved to Ohio."

Although I visited Dr. Learner on at least one other occasion in the nursing care unit, I never managed to compile enough biographical material to produce a true life history. I just didn't have the time.

Although she was an "outlier" in the sense that she had no real friends (other than the nurses and floor staff, all of whom loved her) at the Ponds and was pretty much out of its main stream, she was happy with her memories and the occasional visits from her family. My brief acquaintance with this sweet old lady who had lived life to the fullest was an uplifting experience for me.

And then there was **Manfred**. One afternoon after lunch in the main dining hall, I noticed a small, dapperly dressed man sitting on a bench in a corridor off of the quad. He seemed to be trying to make eye contact with the passing residents, hoping to be noticed. As I approached, he gave me a big smile and a cheerful "hi". Because I sensed that he was looking for someone to talk to, I sat down next to him and introduced myself.

We had a nice chat about the Ponds and its amenities. He told me that he was a new resident, and although he "loved"

164

it here, he was a little intimidated by the sophistication of the residents. And, he said,

> "I retired ten years ago at the age of 75 after many years of service as the head grounds keeper at [the nearby Ivy League] university. My daughter Shelley decided to put me here because of how old I am, and because she thinks I will be happier living with people my own age.
>
> I have a son too; he is a Sergeant in the Cranberry Police Force. And I have a grandson who is both a paramedic and a cop, and another relative who works with the K-9 Corps., involved with drugs."

This was the first of a number impromptu meetings I had with Manfred (he asked me to call him Manfred).

One afternoon I decided to go to the Ponds thrift shop to see who and what was there. I was told that items in the thrift shop were contributed by current Ponds residents as well as by the families of deceased Ponds residents. The proceeds were used mainly to help those individuals who were having difficulty meeting their monthly residence fees and other living expenses. Manfred was there with his daughter Shelley Burns, who was helping him to try on various articles of clothing. He introduced me to his daughter as his "academic friend."

I told Mrs. Burns that I liked Manfred very much and that we talked frequently. I mentioned, kiddingly, that he strategically positioned himself around the hallways so that he could meet everyone on their way to meals. And I also complimented her on how "spiffily" she kept him dressed.

She seemed very happy that her father had made a friend, and she was anxious to confide in me her hopes for

165

Manfred's successful integration into the Ponds community. She said,

> "He buys clothes here to keep up with the Ponds dress protocol. He talks to everyone here, even those who wouldn't otherwise talk to everyone, and he is making the community happier for it. He is a world authority on the [prominent Ivy League University] campus you know."

Manfred was full of jokes and there was no end to his humorous comments about people and situations and life in general. He sometimes referred to the Ponds as the "finishing school", and he claimed that since the average age at the Ponds was 86 (his number, not mine), "I really shouldn't be here." He was fun to be around because he was always upbeat. But, other than the quiet Mr. Sussen, who had become an occasional lunch companion, I almost never saw Manfred in conversation or otherwise actively involved with any of the other residents.

Even though I never overheard any negative comments about him, I did notice that people, except floor staff members who loved him, were very adept at not noticing him. He was from a different socioeconomic background than most of the other residents, and he seemed to be paying the price for it...

As previously mentioned, I had been "warned" by Helene Koster not to assume that all of the residents at the Ponds were either interesting or accomplished. According to Mrs. Koster there was a significant minority here who she referred to as "the dull ones". And right near the top of her list was a woman named **Heather Brown**. I decided to approach Mrs. Brown to see for myself.

One morning while I was looking for the archives storage room, I came upon the slight, stooped lady I knew from her picture in the Ponds residents biography book to be Heather

Brown. In her bio she had listed her former occupation as "secretary". I had seen her almost every day of my stay walking almost everywhere on the premises. After I introduced myself, she told me that she had seen me too, but had thought that I must be part of the staff. When I marveled at the amount of walking she did she said,

> "I much prefer walking to exercise equipment. I used to walk outside before I got here, because I don't like air conditioning. I don't use it at all in my apartment. But now it's a whole different routine. I think of myself as a great explorer. I go all over the place finding what is there and what is going on. I have never owned a cane, and I don't think people would use canes if they didn't have family to tell them how old they are."

I next ran into Mrs. Brown on one of her walks about a week later and asked her if she was willing to give me an interview, or just talk for a little while. She told me,

> "I don't think you should be talking to me because I am not representative of the residents here."

I managed, however, to convince her to sit down with me and to tell me a little bit about herself:

> "I am 93, and I was born in Allegheny. Years ago when I was an applicant to Carnegie Tech I was called personally by Andrew Carnegie, Jr. because I was born in the same place as his family. He offered me free tuition to Carnegie Tech, which is a sort of poor man's Princeton and a rival of Princeton.
>
> I graduated as an office manager, but I was really only a secretary. I have no family at all, just a few friends who visit from the Westfield, Pennsylvania

area, near the Ohio border, where I used to live. I think I have been here for about five years."

 Although she told me she was generally contented with the Ponds, she did feel that those who had to stay on "campus" all of the time including holidays because they had nobody to go visit were being somewhat "short changed".

> "Only about a half dozen or so people without families are here for holiday dinners. I wish management would focus a little more on who is going to be here rather than who is not going to be here, and give us a little more attention."

When I asked Mrs. Brown if she had made friends at the Ponds, her answer was a little vague:

> "I think this is a good place for people without families to come because there are a lot of people to make friends with. I move two chairs so that their backs are against the sectional facing the fireplace in the main resident lounge. That way I am facing the hallway so that I can see people. Sometimes they just wave or yell 'hello', but it makes you feel they are part of the family."

She then pointed to the shell collection on the table across the hall and said,

> "My father used to collect shells. He loved the fact that God spread these pretty little things all over the seashore for people to get."

I wanted to talk more with Mrs. Brown, but I was already late for another scheduled resident interview. When I asked her if we could meet at the site of her favorite chairs the following morning at 8:30 am, she agreed, but asked me again why I wanted to talk to her.

Although I did catch up with Mrs. B. at about 9:00 the following morning, it was not at the designated site, where I had waited for thirty minutes. Instead, she was walking briskly toward the resident's grill; she had completely forgotten our date. She told me that she had some "housework" to do, and I had another interview scheduled at 9:30, so our talk was off for the moment. I told her I would call her. Although we never managed a real interview, we did talk sometimes when we encountered each other in the hallways.

I didn't find Mrs. Brown "dull" at all; I found her charming (albeit in a sort of self-deprecating way). On the one hand, she was a quiet, rather lonely soul with simple tastes and lowered expectations as to her prospects for what Mrs. Koster might think of as a "rich and varied lifestyle". On the other hand though, she found pleasure in exploring all of the nooks and crannies of the Ponds, she enjoyed the occasional company of her former friends, and she loved watching and waving to her fellow residents.

Mrs. Brown seemed content with the quiet, comfortable life which this community afforded, even if most of its other residents never noticed her.

Chapter Ten

Some Concluding Observations
and Some Advice

Due largely to the financial requirements for entrance, the majority of CCRC's are populated by individuals at the upper end of the socio-economic scale; and most CCRC residents are white Caucasians. The Ponds is not an exception to this, and, as is also true of the genre, it offers a highly desirable location, a high quality of service, and an excellent reputation within its sought after demographic.

These qualities, when combined with the word of mouth referrals it receives from its current residents, have provided the Ponds with the ability to attract a particular "quality" of resident and to maintain its standards of gracious living.

Along with its relatively stringent admission requirements, the Ponds has also developed a unique set of protocols which must be adhered to by neophyte residents in order for them to gain full acceptance as members in good standing of the community.

Egalitarianism prevails, for the most part, among those who adhere to these protocols, regardless of their particular social and political affiliations within the group at large. Isolation, to one degree (and in one form) or another, seems to await those who do not follow the protocols. A significant number of the ones who fail to "make the grade" eventually leave the Ponds.

Those who "make the cut" and stay in the community seem to have at least one thing in common: they all wish to somehow simplify their lives. And the majority of individuals who are admitted to the Ponds, are eventually "socialized" into the community by means of their membership in the specific resident organizations they choose to join.

Residents' allegiance is largely to those fellow residents who have similar backgrounds, interests and affiliations (professional, institutional, political, spiritual etc.). They also align themselves with those who similarly utilize the facility's services and amenities, and participate (or not) in its governance.

But, probably most importantly, new residents affiliate with those among their peers who attach the same "meanings" to their choice of the CCRC lifestyle. These meanings will typically boil down to some variation or combination of the following: a.) the CCRC as a chance for a new beginning, b.) the CCRC as a place to die, c.) the CCRC as a guaranteed source of nursing care, d.) the CCRC as a means for alleviating the burden on their children, or e.) the CCRC as a seasonal residence.

Most of the individuals I spoke with at the Ponds had known exactly what to expect when they first came to the place; they had carefully weighed the advantages and disadvantages of the CCRC lifestyle. Many had researched the costs, the bios of the current residents and the amenities; they had compared it to other CCRCs, and they had spent time on the premises. A significant number chose the Ponds over other similarly gracious CCRCs because they had friends who were already residing at the Ponds, and for many, the facility was legitimized in that it had been promoted in their college alumni literature.

In spite of all the due diligence, however, it is not true that everyone at the Ponds was there because they wanted to be. Some - who were there only to avoid being unnecessary burdens to their children or who were there only because they needed medical assistance - missed their large suburban homes and their careers and their ability to drive anywhere they wanted any time they wanted to.

171

Conversely, however, others had come before they "needed" to, and not necessarily to ease their children's burdens. These individuals were anxious to join their cohorts who were also fellow professionals and on an equal socio-economic footing; they were looking for new beginnings in a luxurious, stress-free environment with guaranteed, first rate medical attention when they needed it.

There are, of course, tradeoffs involved with CCRC living which extend beyond the costs. The size of the community dictates a certain regimen. So, for example, even though the food is considered quite good by most, dining must take place at certain times, whether or not those times correspond with the individual's preferences; and residences are comfortable, but space is quite limited. Also, as mentioned before, there are *defacto* codes and protocols - in addition to the "official" rules of the place – pertaining to such things as dress and dining. And finally, new residents must begin all over again in terms of forming friendships.

This book has been written in an attempt to provide for the reader an "insiders" perspective of what life is actually "like" for the residents of a CCRC. Efforts have been made, wherever possible, to convey this sense through the utilization of residents' own dialogue (as opposed to my interpretation of their communications).

And, I have endeavored to add validity to my own interpretations of what was going on through what some social scientists refer to as "triangulation". In simple terms, what the notion of triangulation alleges is the ability to validate the truth of informants statements with a.) observations of their behavior and b.) with statements by other informants regarding the same events or subject matter.

This is not intended as a "how to" guide for deciding for or against the CCRC as a lifestyle. I feel that it is prudent for one to do his or her "homework" with regard to this decision. The first step is weighing the very personal tradeoffs inherent in this lifestyle choice. The second step is to find out more about how the CCRC admission process works and about specific CCRC's. As to the latter, the internet is an invaluable tool.

One very useful publication is *The Consumer's Directory of Continuing Care RetirementCommunities,* which contains a listing of CCRC's throughout the United States with summaries of the services they provide, fee information (there are a number of payment and ownership variations), contracts (an eldercare attorney is recommended here) and so on. This manual is published by the American Association of Homes and Services for the Aging, 901 E Street, NW/Suite 500-Washington, D.C. 200004-2037 (phone: 1-800-508-9442).

The final step in the decision-making process is the visit to the CCRC's of interest (it is prudent to visit at least two). Most CCRC's want the potential resident to be comfortable with his of her decision to move there; turnover can be demoralizing to those already in residence, and administrators want to avoid the paperwork and potentially ill feelings generated by contract termination, the computing and issuing of refunds etc.

 In light of this, many CCRC's will encourage candidates' interaction with residents already there (e.g. a lunch, or a tour of the premises), without the presence of administrative personnel. And some will actually require an overnight stay to provide the prospective new resident with the full flavor of everything the place has to offer.

Make no mistake, however, those seeking residence will be evaluated by the CCRC too, in terms of, among other things, how well they fit the facility's "image" of the successful resident, what their state of health is, and the adequacy of their financial circumstances.

Printed in the United States
40095LVS00002B/52